H. EDWARD FLEMING
Florida Community College at Jacksonville

STUDY GUIDE TO ACCOMPANY
AMERICAN GOVERNMENT

FIFTH EDITION

WALTER E. VOLKOMER
Hunter College of the City University of New York

with the editorial assitance of Carolyn D. Smith

D1379043

Prentice-Hall, Englewood Cliffs, New Jersey 07632

Editorial/production supervision and
   interior design: John A. Nestor
Manufacturing buyer: Peter Havens

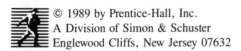
Printed in the United States of America

10 9 8 7 6 5 4 3 2 1

ISBN 0-13-027376-7

Prentice-Hall International (UK) Limited, *London*
Prentice-Hall of Australia Pty. Limited, *Sydney*
Prentice-Hall Canada Inc., *Toronto*
Prentice-Hall Hispanoamericana, S.A., *Mexico*
Prentice-Hall of India Private Limited, *New Delhi*
Prentice-Hall of Japan, Inc., *Tokyo*
Simon & Schuster Asia Pte. Ltd., *Singapore*
Editora Prentice-Hall do Brasil, Ltda., *Rio de Janeiro*

CONTENTS

PREFACE

This Study Guide has been written as a supplement to American Government, fifth edition, by Walter E. Volkomer. The intent of this work is to assist students in mastering basic information about the American political system.

Study guides can be very useful in preparing students for knowledge of course material. They can be used to reinforce the textbook and also can provide immediate feedback about how well one understands textbook themes and factual information.

Although intended for students, a project of this nature forces a writer to review basic themes, topics, and factual information in subject matter and to evaluate how to communicate the material to students. Such a review may be refreshing and beneficial, both professionally and personally.

I wish to take this opportunity to express my gratitude to those close to me who have made this possible. Ken Bateh is a friend who taught me how to use my computer in this project and Carol Craig is a special person whose love and assistance saw me through this. Melanie Fleming and Cliff Fleming have special meaning in this as well.

St. Augustine, Florida

H. Edward Fleming

NOTE TO THE STUDENT

One may gain a basic understanding and knowledge of the American political system through the combined use of the Study Guide and the book <u>American Government</u>. The Study Guide supplements the textbook and there is a chapter in the Study Guide for each chapter in the text.

Each chapter of the Study Guide has a similar organizational structure. A <u>chapter overview</u> begins each chapter and gives a brief description of the chapter material in the text. <u>Learning objectives</u> help identify significant topics and themes in each chapter. A <u>chapter outline</u> further highlights key topics, terms, and concepts. This is followed by a <u>chapter summary</u> which provides a review of the chapter material. Next a series of <u>practice exercises</u> are available to assist the student in assessing how well the material has been mastered. The practice exercises consist of thirty questions. There are always ten each of completion and multiple choice questions, five true false questions, and five discussion or essay questions.

The Study Guide is to assist the student, and must be used in conjunction with the book <u>American Government</u> for a student to master the material. A glossary in the text is very valuable and should be used whenever the student needs a key political term defined.

A student should study course material systematically and consistently for the most comprehensive knowledge of the material. The best use of the Study Guide is made by a student who will read the textbook assignment and identify the chapter themes, topics, and factual information. Next the student should use the Study Guide to analyze how well the material is mastered. The short answer questions should provide some indication of how well specific factual information is known and the essay questions may be used to determine how well chapter themes and topics are understood. Remember, there is no substitute for reading the text.

1 POLITICS DEMOCRACY, AND THE AMERICAN PEOPLE

CHAPTER OVERVIEW

Chapter 1 of American Government establishes basic concepts that are important in understanding the foundations of the American political system. The nature of politics is examined and concepts of politics, power, legitimacy, and government are developed.

This chapter also provides an explanation of a political system and places democracy within this context while identifying and describing principles associated with democracy.

The chapter concluds with a discussion of democracy and diversity, that suggests diversity in a democracy creates tensions which make agreement on solutions to political problems difficult.

LEARNING OBJECTIVES

1. Identify, describe, and define basic concepts and terms necessary for the study of American democracy and the American political system.

2. Recognize and comprehend two contrasting views of political power in America.

3. Understand the concept of democracy and a political system.

4. List and explain bases of American democracy.

5. Examine and understand the political theories of significant political philosophers who contributed to American democratic and constitutional development.

1

LEARNING OBJECTIVES (cont.)

6. Analyze sources of diversity in American society and relate the impact of diversity to the complexity of American politics.

CHAPTER OUTLINE

I. The Nature of Politics
   A. Concepts of politics
   B. Relationship of politics and power
   C. Power in America: pluralism or elitism
   D. Legitimate power: tradition, charisma and law
   E. Politics and government

II. The Concept of a Political System
   A. The function of a political system
   B. The product of a political system

III. Democracy as a Political System
   A. Definition of a democracy
      1. Representative democracy
      2. Direct democracy
   B. Bases of democracy
      1. Self-government
      2. Social contract
      3. Majority rule
      4. Minority rights
      5. Limited government
      6. Equality
      7. Democratic institutions
      8. Free elections
      9. Organized opposition
      10. Free expression of ideas
      11. Universal education

IV. Democracy and Diversity
   A. A heterogeneous society with racial, ethnic, and religious diversity
   B. A diverse society with multiple, complex political problems.

V. Conclusions
   A. Citizen freedom from arbitrary rule
   B. Survival of the American Creed
   C. Institutional stress, societal problems, and democratic failures

2

CHAPTER SUMMARY

The introductory chapter of this text on American government begins appropriately with an explanation of politics, a political system, democracy, principles of democracy, and provides an introduction to the American political system.

Several definitions of politics are given, ranging from the cynical to the ideal, and the relationship between politics and power is clearly established in all areas of human life. Also political power in America is presented as either pluralistic or elitist in nature and the concept of the legitimate exercise of power is explained in terms of tradition, charisma, and legality. This concept leads to a distinction being made between politics and government.

The concept of a political system is presented with political democracy defined in terms of either representative democracy or direct democracy. There are several principles associated with all forms of democracy and these are carefully and clearly described.

Democracy in the United States is also characterized with significant diversity easily seen in the racial/ethnic and religious composition of the U.S. population. Such diversity produces a wide range of opinions on political topics and makes political agreements on significant issues difficult to obtain. These are some of the complexities of political democracies.

Regardless of the tensions and difficulties of democracy, the American political system is based on freedom of the citizen from arbitrary rule, and an American Creed that embraces constitutionalism, lawful rule of government, equality, individualism, and democracy.

PRACTICE EXERCISES

FILL IN THE BLANKS

1. Political scientist Harold Lasswell described politics as_____ _____ _____, _____, ____ _____.

2. _____ is a view that political power in the United States is dispersed among many individuals and groups whereas an argument that political power is concentrated in the hands of a few refers to _____.

3

FILL IN THE BLANKS (cont.)

3. The term _____ _____ refers to each voter personally and directly deciding governmental issues.

4. The _____ _____ theory of government maintains that people make a fundamental agreement creating a political community and government.

5. The basic elements of the "_____ _____" as stated by Samuel P. Huntington are: liberty, equality, individualism, democracy, and the rule of law under a constitution."

6. Legitimacy in politics comes from _____ _____ _____.

7. Rules, laws, administrative and judicial decisions, and treaties which are products of the political system are the products of the political system and are known as _____ _____.

8. Representative democracy is also called _____ _____ because people are represented by officials who make political decisions for them.

9. The ability of people to govern themselves is called _____-_____.

10. _____ means freedom to express one's opinions.

MULTIPLE CHOICE

11. Three of the following are definitions of politics; which is not?
    a. Who gets what, when and how.
    b. A process by which values are authoritatively allocated for society.
    c. The art of governing humanity by deceiving it.
    d. The institutions and processes by which rules are made and enforced for all in society.
    e. Charisma

12. The ability to influence the political behavior of others is called:
    a. Pluralism
    b. Political power
    c. Government
    d. Charisma

4

MULTIPLE CHOICE (cont.)

13. Regularly scheduled elections, political parties, and freedom to discuss political ideas are all characteristics of:
    a. Representative democracy
    b. Universal education
    c. Direct democracy
    d. The rule of law

14. The importance of charisma as a source of political legitimacy reflects on an emphasis on:
    a. Law
    b. Tradition
    c. Rules
    d. Personality

15. The author of Democracy In America, an analysis of the American political system was:
    a. John Locke
    b. Max Weber
    c. Alexis de Tocqueville
    d. Thomas Jefferson

16. The idea that the powers of government should be limited and embodied in a basic law refers to:
    a. Diversity
    b. Constitutionalism
    c. Pluralism
    d. Self-government

17. The view that powerful individuals maintain significant positions in finance, industry, government and the military and rule society refers to:
    a. Self-government
    b. Elitism
    c. Charisma
    d. Legitimacy

18. Philosophical views on natural law, natural rights, the social contract, limited government, and government protection of man's rights are the cornerstone of American democracy. Which of the following political philosophers expressed this philosophy?
    a. John Locke
    b. Jean Jacques Rousseau
    c. Alexis de Tocqueville
    d. Max Weber

5

MULTIPLE CHOICE (cont.)

19. Historically, equality as a democratic value has meant:
    a. Substantial economic equality
    b. Political and legal equality
    c. Choosing equality at the expense of liberty
    d. Choosing economic equality over political equality

20. Which of the following political philosophers is not recognized as having made a significant contribution to the American constitutional system?
    a. James Madison
    b. Baron de Montesquieu
    c. John Locke
    d. Karl Marx

TRUE OR FALSE

21. The popularity of personal leadership is called charisma. _____

22. Elected representatives making public policy is an example of direct democracy. _____

23. Public policy is regarded as the product of a political system. _____

24. Elections promote stability and order in society. _____

25. The view that a small group of wealthy, powerful individuals rule American society is called pluralism. _____

DISCUSSION, ESSAY

I. Define democracy and explain the bases of democracy.

II. Examine sources of diversity in American society and describe how diversity complicates political democracy in America.

III. Discuss significant philosophical contributions to American democracy of John Locke and Baron de Montesquieu.

DISCUSSION, ESSAY (cont.)

IV. Discuss significant philosophical contributions of Thomas Jefferson and James Madison to American democratic ideals and constitutional development.

V. Examine the concept of equality from different perspectives and explain Thomas Jefferson's view of equality. What is your concept of equality?

2 FROM COLONIALISM TO CONSTITUTONALISM

CHAPTER OVERVIEW

Chapter 2 develops several prominent themes in American political history. In the colonial period attention is given to the significance of the English legal system taking root in the colonies and the inheritance of the English emphasis on individual rights. The struggle of the colonists against Parliamentary authority is described and the colonial period ends with the Declaration of Independence.

The struggle of the newly independent states for constitutional rule is stressed as the Articles of Confederation are examined and the turmoil of the time ultimately forces a re-examination of the framework of government.

Features of the U.S. Constitution are described and the chapter concludes with a discussion of how the Constitution has been able to endure for two centuries with lasting principles while yet providing flexibility to adapt to changing needs of society.

LEARNING OBJECTIVES

1. Recognize and understand political developments from the colonial period to the Articles of Confederation.

2. Analyze the defects of the Articles of Confederation.

3. Understand the causes of Shay's Rebellion.

4. Describe conflicts and compromises at the Constitutional Convention.

LEARNING OBJECTIVES (cont.)
5. Examine principles of the U.S. Constitution.

6. Distinguish between formal amending procedures of the U.S. Constitution and informal means of constitutional interpretation.

7. Grasp how our constitution is a "living constitution" that establishes continuity and yet provides flexibility for a changing society.

8. Define and understand new terms and concepts introduced in the chapter.

CHAPTER OUTLINE

I. The Road to Independence
   A. The English heritage of law and individual rights
   B. Colonial cooperation
   C. The First Continental Congress
   D. The Revolution
   E. The Declaration of Independence and the Second Continental Congress

II. The Articles of Confederation
   A. Government under the Articles
   B. Shay's Rebellion

III. The Constitutional Convention
   A. Delegates
   B. Issues
   C. Ratification

IV. Constitutional Principles
   A. Federalism
   B. Separation of powers
   C. Checks and balances
   D. National Supremacy
   E. Judicial Review

V. Constitutional change and development
   A. Formal amending procedures
   B. Experience, practice and interpretation

VI. Conclusions
   A. Enduring principles
   B. Flexibility and continuity

CHAPTER SUMMARY

The United States Constitution is concluding its second century as a foundation for government in this country and has demonstrated remarkable adaptability as a basic instrument of governance.

The struggle for legal rights and constitutional development in this country can be described in several distinct phases. The first phase describes a colonial period in which the English legal system and English emphasis on individual rights is inherited by the colonies. Yet, this phase also involves colonial struggle, first against Indians and later against England as the colonists cooperated to establish and clarify their rights within the English colonial system. Eventually this phase ended in a successful struggle for independence from Great Britain which is symbolized by the Declaration of Independence.

The second phase of the struggle for constitutionalism was the struggle for a structure of government after independence. The first constitutional structure established, the Articles of Confederation, proved unworkable in the face of economic turmoil and fear of granting power to a centralized government. This phase ended with the specter of popular insurrection in western Massachusetts over economic ills and recognition by political leaders that the Articles were incapable of providing a framework of unified constitutional government among the thirteen states.

The third phase began with the Constitutional Convention of May 1787. This convention was authorized by Congress to revise the Articles of Confederation. The convention delegates were established and respected political leaders who saw the issues requiring a new constitutional framework with stronger powers for a national government. The convention worked out a series of basic compromises over government that were accepted by most delegates in September 1787, thus the United States Constitution was completed in basic form and attention now shifted to a struggle to obtain the adoption of the document by the states.

The struggle to obtain constitutional approval was fought in state ratification conventions as provided for in the new document. Delegates were elected by the voters in each state to attend state conventions where the pros and cons of the document were debated. Those who supported the Constitution were called Federalists and their opponents were labeled Antifederalists.

CHAPTER SUMMARY (cont.)

After several months, conventions in most states ratified the document. Yet, in some states bitter battles ensued and promises of amendments eventually secured adoption of the Constitution. In 1789 the new U.S. Constitution became effective.

The Constitution is a document establishing limited powers for government. Various constitutional principles to limit governmental power have proved lasting over the past two centuries and include federalism, separation of powers, checks and balances, national supremacy, and judicial review.

The United State Constitutional system has proven to be lasting and provide stability while yet permitting formal and informal methods of constitutional change. The formal procedures of constitutional change involve a two step process of proposing and ratifying amendments which have resulted in twenty-six formal changes to the document. Also, informal means of constitutional development, experience and accepted practice, have become established as our constitutional system has evolved. The development of political parties, the institution of the cabinet, and the impact of U.S. Supreme Court decisions all have given meaning to our Constitution as a "living constitution."

In conclusion, one can state that the U.S. constitutional system is a system which has basic enduring principles of government and has provided flexibility and continuity for two centuries.

PRACTICE EXERCISES

FILL IN THE BLANKS

1. The _____ _____ _____ _____ of 1689 established basic rights for Englishmen as trial by jury and the right to petition government.

2. The _____ _____ _____ adopted the Declaration of Independence which formalized the colonial breakaway from Great Britain.

3. The first written constitutional framework of government for the United States was the _____ _____ _____.

FILL IN THE BLANKS (cont.)

4. The insurrection in Massachusetts in 1786 against state courts because of mortgage foreclosures on farms was known as _____ _____.

5. The initial plan presented at the Constitutional Convention which was the basis for beginning the proceedings of the convention was the _____

6. The Constitutional Convention adopted the _____ _____ as a basis for a bicameral legislative body called Congress.

7. A system of organizing government based on geographic division of power is called _____.

8. _____ _____ refers to the power of courts to declare legislative and executive actions of government unconstitutional.

9. The dependency of one branch of government on another refers to _____ _____.

10. The _____ _____ were a collection of eighty-five essays written by three leading proponents of the U. S. Constitution.

MULTIPLE CHOICE

11. The constitutional system of establishing clear and distinct branches of government is called:
   a) supremacy of national law
   b) federalism
   c) separation of powers
   d) representative democracy

12. Two informal means of constitutional development include:
   a) amendment and lawmaking
   b) experience and accepted practice
   c) treatymaking and amendment
   d) lawmaking and experience

13. An act adopted by the British Parliament in 1764 which levied import duties on wines, coffee, and other commodities in order to raise revenue from the colonies was:
   a) the American Revenue Act (Sugar Act)
   b) the Stamp Act
   c) The Tea Act
   d) the Coercive Acts

MULTIPLE CHOICE (cont.)

14. A compromise adopted by the Constitutional Convention which permitted slave holding states to partially count slaves so to increase representation in the House of Representatives was:
   a) the commerce compromise
   b) the three-fifths compromise
   c) the treaty ratification compromise
   d) the Virginia Plan

15. Those who opposed ratification of the U.S. Constitution and worked to defeat it in the ratification conventions were called:
   a) federalists
   b) nationalists
   c) confederationists
   d) antifederalists

16. Which of the following institutions declared independence of the United States from Great Britain?
   1) the Second Continental Congress
   2) the First Continental Congress
   3) the Correspondence Committees
   4) the British Parliament

17. Which of the following devices is not found in the U.S. Constitution?
   1) federalism
   2) separation of powers and checks and balances
   3) monarchy
   4) national supremacy and judicial review

18. Opponents of the Constitution criticized the document very effectively for its failure:
   a) to prohibit ex post facto laws
   b) to include a list of individual rights
   c) to prohibit bills of attainder
   d) to provide for a writ of habeas corpus

19. A European who traveled to the United States and examined the American political system and commented on the American expression of democracy was:
   a) Thomas Paine
   b) Alexander Hamilton
   c) Alexandre von Homboldt
   d) Alexis de Tocqueville

MULTIPLE CHOICE (cont.)

20. A general description of the delegates at the Constitutional Convention would be that as a group:
    a) they were well educated and politically experienced
    b) they were average Americans and middle class
    c) they were frontiersmen and lower social class
    d) they were representative of women and blacks

TRUE OR FALSE

21. Delegates at the Constitutional Convention were popularly elected. _____

22. One of the earliest reasons for colonial cooperation was the threat of Indians, French and Dutch attacks on English colonies. _____

23. The Articles of Confederation failed because they provided too little authority for the central government to tax or regulate commerce. _____

24. Bills of attainder are permitted under the U.S. Constitution. _____

25. The U.S. Constitution was adopted by popular vote of the citizens of states. _____

DISCUSSION, ESSAY

I. Briefly identify and explain major compromises of the Constitutional Convention.

II. Briefly identify, explain, or describe the following:
    Shay's Rebellion
    The Federalists Papers
    The Albany Plan
    The Articles of Confederation
    The Bill of Rights

III. Describe the various procedures by which the United States Constitution may be amended.

IV. Discuss principles in the U.S. Constitution which gives meaning to the concept of limited government.

V. Explain the concept of constitutional development and include in your answer how our constitution is considered a living constitution that provides flexibility and continuity.

14

3 THE FEDERAL SYSTEM

CHAPTER OVERVIEW

The United States Constitution establishes a federal system of government that has been the basis for federal-state relationships for two hundred years. Federal-state relationships have undergone significant changes over two centuries but the enduring principles of American federalism remain: shared powers between national and state governments, reserved powers to states, prohibited powers to both governments and national government obligations to states in the union.

As society has grown and changed and succeeding generations have sought to redefine governmental responsibilities, the federal nature of the American political system has provided continuity while undergoing change itself. Many of the different directions of American federalism are presented along with mention of specific grant programs that characterize growth and development in the American federal system of government.

LEARNING OBJECTIVES

1. Define and understand new terms and concepts introduced in the study of the federal system.

2. Define the concepts of federal, unitary, and confederation governments.

3. Understand the concept of federalism in the American political system.

4. Identify powers of the federal and state governments in the American political system.

LEARNING OBJECTIVES (cont.)

5. Recognize limitations and obligations of both state and federal governments.

6. Explain constitutional guarantees of relations among states in the union.

7. Understand the constitutional basis of national supremacy in the American political system.

8. Examine theories of federalism.

9. Trace the history of federalism in the American political system.

CHAPTER OUTLINE

I. Federalism as a Governmental System
   A. Comparative systems: federalism, unitary, or confederation
   B. Divided powers of federalism

II. Federalism in the Constitution
   A. Historical development: confederation and federalism
   B. Powers of the U.S. Government
      1. Delegated powers
      2. Implied powers
   C. Concurrent powers
      1. Taxing and spending power
      2. Borrowing money
      3. Eminent domain
      4. Establish courts
      5. Enforce law
   D. Limitations on national government
      1. Prohibitions on bill of attainder
      2. Prohibitions on **ex post facto laws**
      3. Limited suspension of **writs of habeas corpus**
      4. Constitutional guarantees of Bill of Rights
   E. Limitations on state governments
      1. Exercise of reserve powers
      2. Prohibitions of U.S. Constitution
      3. Limitations imposed by U.S. constitutional amendments
   F. Interstate relations among states
      1. "Full faith and credit" clause of the U.S. Constitution
      2. "Privileges and immunities" clause of the U.S. Constitution

16

CHAPTER OUTLINE (cont.)

    3. "Interstate rendition" clause of U.S. Constitution
    4. Interstate compacts authorized by U.S. Constitution
    5. U.S. Supreme Court jurisdiction

III. Governmental Obligations in Federalism
  A. National obligations to states
    1. Republican form of government
    2. Protect states against foreign invasion
    3. Protect states against domestic violence
  B. State obligations
    1. Maintain republican government
    2. Preserve domestic peace
    3. Elect members of Congress
    4. Fill vacancies in state Congressional delegations
    5. Select presidential electoral college delegates
    6. Consider U.S. Constitutional amendment proposals

IV. National Supremacy in Federalism
  A. Constitutional requirement of Article VI of Constitution
  B. U.S. Supreme Court umpire of the Constitution

V. Theories and Practices of Federalism
  A. Competitive federalism
    1. Nation centered federalism
    2. State centered federalism
    3. Dual federalism
  B. Cooperative federalism
    1. Cooperative federal-state activities
    2. Federal competitive grants-in-aid
      a. Category grants
      b. Matching grants
  C. Creative federalism
  D. Nixon's "New Federalism"
    1. General revenue sharing
    2. Block grants
  E. Reagan's "New Federalism"
    1. Reduce federal spending
      a. Consolidate block grants
      b. Reduce revenue sharing
    2. Greater state responsibilities
      a. More state revenues required
      b. End revenue sharing

CHAPTER SUMMARY

The American political system is a federal system of government which divides power between a national government and state governments. The federal system of government in the United States means that most citizens are under jurisdictions of local government, state government, and the federal government.

Our federal system contrasts sharply to unitary governments which place most power in a central government, or a confederation in which states narrowly grant authority to a central government.

Federalism in the United States is structured by the U.S. Constitution which establishes a national government of delegated powers and implied powers while permitting the sharing of powers by both the federal and state levels of government. In addition, states exercise reserved powers under our Constitution while some powers are prohibited to both levels of government.

Sources of delegated and implied powers of the federal government are the U.S. Constitution and important judicial decisions of the U.S. Supreme Court.

Our Constitution also permits both federal and state governments to exercise certain powers concurrently, as taxing and spending powers, while the Constitution also places prohibitions on certain powers at the national level of government and state government.

Relations among states in the union are authorized by the Constitution in Article IV, while Article I permits states to establish interstate compacts with Congressional approval.

The Constitution also requires obligations of both the federal and state governments in our union. The federal government has obligations to guarantee the republican nature of state governments and protect states against foreign invasion and domestic violence, while states are obligated to maintain republican governments and domestic peace. States must also participate fully in their obligations to maintain representation in the federal level of government, including representation in Congress, the Presidential election process, and consider amendments to the U.S. Constitution.

CHAPTER SUMMARY (cont.)

The federal system established by our Constitution provides distinctions between federal and state powers and obligations and provides that the national government has supremacy in its area of policymaking through Article VI of the Constitution. Additionally, the U.S. Supreme Court, under the Constitution has assumed a responsibility as umpire in federal-state conflicts.

The practice and theory of federalism has varied in the history of our constitutional system. Early in the development of our federal system a theory of national centered federalism suggested that the federal government was supreme in a federal-state conflict while there also emerged a strong contrasting belief that the federal union should be state centered because state delegations wrote the Constitution and state ratifying conventions approved the document. This concept envisioned only narrowly delegated powers to the federal government. However, the concept of federalism that served the nation from the nineteenth century into the twentieth century was the theory of dual federalism which held that each government was supreme in its own area of policymaking. The effect of this theory was to build up state authority, often at the expense of the national government.

The twentieth century gave rise to new views of federalism as the resources of the national government were necessary to meet demands for new government services at state and local levels of government. Cooperative federalism emerged and envisioned the federal and state governments as partners to provide services. Numerous federal grant programs were established to foster cooperative federal-state policies to provide governmental services.

Eventually, by the 1960's, the civil rights struggle forced the federal government to assume a larger and more forceful role in coercing states to support a wider range of domestic policies than states may have desired. This expanded federal role is referred to as creative federalism. This was followed in the 1970's and 1980's by "new federalism" initiated by President Nixon. This "new federalism" developed revenue sharing and block grants and let states have greater discretion in uses of federal monies. By the 1980's, President Reagan's "new federalism" sought to reduce federal spending and promote greater state responsibility in domestic policymaking. The result in federal-state relations has been to eliminate revenue sharing, reduce federal grant programs, and use block grants to permit states to address their problems. Whether Reagan's approach is continued only time will tell.

PRACTICE EXERCISES

FILL IN THE BLANKS

1. In a _____ system of government, the central government grants specific powers to local governments.

2. Immediately prior to the Constitution becoming the basis of government in the United States, the U.S. had a _____ form of government.

3. In the _____ ____ _____ case, the U.S. Supreme Court upheld the broad authority of Congress to exercise implied powers to create a banking system.

4. _____ _____ _____ are legislative enactments which punish individuals without trial. These laws are prohibited by the U.S. Constitution.

5. States exercise _____ _____ under the Tenth Amendment to the U.S. Constitution.

6. A theory of federalism which held each separate level of government was supreme in its areas of jurisdiction is called _____.

7. The forceful use of federal grants to states by the federal government under Lyndon Johnson's administration was referred to as "_____ _____".

8. A sum of money given for a broad general purpose by the federal government to states is called a _____ _____.

9. The returning of federal tax monies, with no strings attached, to the states is called _____ _____ _____.

10. Agreements between states which are approved by Congress are often used to deal with issues between or among states. Such agreements are called _____ _____.

MULTIPLE CHOICE

11. The constitutional division of power between two levels of government refers to which of the following systems of government?
   a. Unitary
   b. Federal
   c. Confederation
   d. Empire

12. Which of the following types of powers are exercised by governments in the United States?
   a. Prohibited, concurrent, implied
   b. Implied, concurrent, delegated
   c. Implied, concurrent, prohibited
   d. Reserve, delegated, implied, concurrent

13. States in the union exercise which of the following types of powers:
   a. Reserved and concurrent
   b. Delegated and reserved
   c. Concurrent and delegated
   d. Implied and prohibited

14. Article IV of the Constitution contains a number of guarantees to states in the union. Which of the following is not found under Article IV?
   a. "Interstate rendition"
   b. "Privileges and immunities" clause
   c. "Interstate compacts"
   d. "Full faith and credit" clause

15. Alexander Hamilton proposed which of the following types of federalism?
   a. Dual federalism
   b. State centered federalism
   c. Cooperative federalism
   d. Nation centered federalism

16. Which of the following types of federal money sharing programs was not a form of grant program under cooperative federalism?
   a. Revenue sharing
   b. Category grants in aid
   c. Matching grants
   d. Competitive grants

17. "New Federalism" under President Reagan emphasizes:
   a. An expanded federal role and revenue sharing
   b. More category grants-in-aid and less money
   c. A reduced federal role and block grants
   d. Enhanced revenue sharing and category grants

MULTIPLE CHOICE (cont.)

18. Specific powers granted to the national government are called:
    a. Implied powers
    b. Delegated powers
    c. Concurrent powers
    d. Reserved powers

19. Those powers which are shared between both states and the federal government are:
    a. Implied powers
    b. Delegated powers
    c. Concurrent powers
    d. Reserved powers

20. Examples of prohibited powers are:
    a. Budget reduction laws and block grants
    b. Interstate compacts and ex post facto laws
    c. Revenue sharing and concurrent powers
    d. Ex post facto laws and bills of attainder

TRUE OR FALSE

21. One major aim of the Reagan administration has been to reduce federal spending in grant programs. _____

22. Revenue sharing and block grants are the same grant program. _____

23. Article VI of the Constitution establishes states supremacy in federal-state conflicts. _____

24. States are guaranteed a republican government under the Constitution. _____

25. Often the U.S. Supreme Court acts as an umpire for conflicts in the federal system. _____

DISCUSSION, ESSAY

I. Distinguish between unitary, federal, and confederation systems of government.

II. Discuss the powers of the federal and state government.

III. Compare and contrast obligations of the federal and state governments under the Constitution.

22

4 PUBLIC OPINION AND VOTING

CHAPTER OVERVIEW

This chapter explores a number of topics that develop an understanding of public opinion and voting behavior in American politics.

Sources of political socialization are described and a relationship is established between political attitudes that people develop and the ability to measure those attitudes. It has also become apparent that television has had a significant impact on influencing public opinion and has contributed to the decline of political parties.

The democratization of the American electorate is traced and a current analysis of the American electorate is provided. The chapter concludes with a recognition that voters today are more independent in making their choices and better educated than in the past.

LEARNING OBJECTIVES

1. Define and understand new terms and concepts introduced in the chapter on public opinion and voting.

2. Define socialization and describe influences that are important in the process of political socialization.

3. Define political opinion and examine features of political opinion.

4. Explain how political opinion polls are developed.

5. Examine criticisms of public opinion polls.

LEARNING OBJECTIVES (cont.)

6. Analyze the role of the media in influencing public opinion and on political campaigns.

7. Recognize the significance of the media in transforming political campaigns and weakening party relationships with American voters.

8. Analyze characteristics of political participants and non-participants in the political process.

CHAPTER OUTLINE

I. The American Political Culture
   A. A democratic political culture
   B. Political leadership commitment to democracy

II. Political Socialization
   A. A definition
   B. Influences affecting political beliefs
      1. Family
      2. School
      3. Peer group
      4. Social class, income, occupation, education
      5. Race, religion
      6. Residence
      7. Political and historical events

III. The Nature of Public Opinion
   A. General features
      1. Intensity
      2. Concentration
      3. Stability
      4. Distribution
      5. Salience
   B. Measuring Public Opinion
      1. Political dialogue with people
      2. Letters to political leaders
      3. Public opinion polls
   C. Public Opinion Polls
      1. Scientific polling
      2. Polling organizations
      3. Clients of opinion polls
   D. Conducting Polls
      1. Sampling
      2. Survey research

CHAPTER OUTLINE (cont.)

    E. Criticisms
       1. Lack accuracy
       2. Published results effect campaigns
       3. Discourages potential voters
       4. Bandwagon effect

IV. The Role of the Media
    A. Agenda setting
    B. Media impact on political communication
    C. Recent trends

V. How Americans Participate
    A. Lower social class people participate less
    B. Higher social class people participate more

VI. The Changing American Voter
    A. Historical evolution
       1. White male suffrage
       2. Women's suffrage
       3. Black suffrage
       4. Lowering the voting age
    B. Who votes today
       1. More people in presidential elections
       2. Fewer people in congressional elections
       3. Well informed, middle aged people vote
       4. Young, disinterested, poorly educated vote less
    C. How people vote
       1. Well educated, higher incomes, Protestants vote Republican
       2. Lower educated, lower income, religious-racial minorities vote Democrat
    D. Partisanship voting declines
       1. Candidate and issues more important today
       2. Party allegiance declining

VII. Conclusions
    A. Dependent voters reflect social force/party loyalty
    B. Responsive voters reflect candidates/issue focus

CHAPTER SUMMARY

The American political culture is a political culture which reflects democratic values of equality, individual freedom, and due process of law and these values are emphasized in the political process. The passage of these values from one

CHAPTER SUMMARY (cont.)

generation to the next is through political socialization which begins in the family. These values reflects personal relationships as well as occupational and more distant social category influences.

The political attitudes that people develop often generate political opinions on a range of issues that are important to political leaders and candidates for public office. These opinions are surveyed scientifically by public opinion polls which are generally regarded as important, but are often criticized as lacking accuracy and distorting election results.

It has become evident that television exerts enormous influence on politics and strongly affects public opinion. Media influence ranges from replacing political parties in reaching out to voters to determining what is newsworthy and increasing a political candidate's dependency on media's outreach potential. There are even accusations that media reports of polling results affect voter turnout.

Americans generally have a rather poor record of political involvement and evidence suggests that citizen involvement in politics is related to social status in society. The right to vote has been extended over the past two centuries, after significant struggles, so that today we have universal adult suffrage. Yet, despite the opportunity for universal citizen involvement, voter participation in presidential elections is barely over 50% while voting in congressional elections is much lower.

A further analysis of citizen participation in politics reveals that a correlation exists between education, income, residence, racial or religious identification and political party support. Citizens with higher educational levels, higher incomes, rural and suburban residences, whites, Protestants, westerners, (and southerners in Presidential elections) tend to support the Republican party. Citizens with lower educational levels, lower incomes, urban residents, racial minorities, union members, southerners (in congressional and state elections) and religious minorities tend to support the Democratic party. These correlations indicate that our political parties in reality are coalitions of voters groups.

Among scholars there have emerged two views of typical voters. The dependent-voter theory maintains that many voters are passive and make up their minds long before

CHAPTER SUMMARY (cont.)

campaigns begin and vote based on party loyalties or social forces, rarely exercising independent judgment. However, a responsive-voter theory suggests that voters make independent voting judgments based on candidates and issues. Dr. Volkomer concludes that voters today are probably more candidate - and issue - oriented and this best explains how people vote.

PRACTICE EXERCISES

FILL IN THE BLANKS

1. The basic values that underlie American life and establish a legitimacy for the American political system are defined as _____ _____.

2. _____ _____ refers to transmitting political values from one generation to another.

3. The opinions expressed by people on a range of political issues is called _____ _____.

4. How strongly an opinion is held is called _____.

5. The selection of a small number of people to study information about a larger group is called a_____.

6. In the _____ ___ _____ case, the U. S. Supreme Court ruled that Congress could only lower voting age to eighteen in Federal elections.

7. It is often believed that an announcement of public opinion results may affect an election outcome. This is called the _____ effect.

8. _____ _____ describes the media's ability to establish issues of public concern.

9. The _____-_____ Amendment to the Constitution lowered the voting age to eighteen in all elections.

10. An argument that voters choose candidates based on issue knowledge and candidate views on issues is called a _____-_____ portrait.

27

MULTIPLE CHOICE

11. Possibly the most powerful influence in shaping political attitudes is:
   a. Social class background
   b. Educational level
   c. Residence
   d. Family

12. Holding the same opinion over a long period of time best describes:
   a. Concentration
   b. Stability
   c. Intensity
   d. Salience

13. Holding strong opinions on an issue or issues is called:
   a. Concentration
   b. Stability
   c. Intensity
   d. Salience

14. Voters in some voting precincts are polled by television news and campaign organizations on election day and the results are used to project campaign results. Such districts are called:
   a. Multipurpose districts
   b. Bellwether districts
   c. Special purpose districts
   d. Registration districts

15. A new method of using television to reach voters in 1988 has been through:
   a. Candidates using other candidates speeches
   b. Candidates having celebrities speak
   c. Video parties
   d. Thirty second campaign messages

16. It is suggested that in political participation among the American people:
   a. Those of higher social class participate more
   b. Those of lower social class participate more
   c. Those of higher social class participate less
   d. There seems to be no relationship to social class participation

17. Voter turnout is usually higher:
   a. In congressional elections
   b. In presidential elections
   c. In the legislative elections
   d. In local elections

MULTIPLE CHOICE (cont.)

18. Which of the following groups tend to vote less often?
    A. Whites, women and the elderly
    b. Non-whites, youth and the poor
    c. Whites, men and the wealthy
    d. Non-whites, youth and the wealthy

19. Most clients for public opinion polls are:
    a. Newspapers
    b. Average voters
    c. Academicians
    d. Politicians and candidates

20. Today voters in the United States:
    a. Depend more on television for information
    b. Are intensely involved in politics
    c. Follow their political party recommendations
    d. Are more likely to vote in local elections

TRUE OR FALSE

21. The dependent-voter is often influenced by social forces and party loyalty. _____

22. The responsive-voter is often influenced by social forces and party loyalty. _____

23. U. S. voter turnout is usually higher than in other democracies. _____

24. Historically Catholics and Jews have supported the Democratic party. _____

25. Today party loyalty among voters is strengthening._____

DISCUSSION, ESSAY

I. Discuss influences that are important in the process of political socialization.

II. Define public opinion and explain the features of public opinion polls.

III. Evaluate criticisms of public opinion polls.

IV. Assess the role of the media in transforming political campaigns and weakening political party relationships with American voters.

DISCUSSION, ESSAY (cont.)

V. Establish profiles of citizen participants and non-participants in the political process and relate these profiles to voter coalitions supportive of the Democratic and Republican parties.

5 POLITICAL PARTIES AND INTEREST GROUPS

CHAPTER OVERVIEW

This chapter examines two organized groups directly involved in influencing public policy: political parties and interest groups. Political parties are distinguished from interest groups in several ways, perhaps the most prominent being that political parties contest elections and organize government. However, interest groups generally have a more narrow focus of interest than political parties, support or oppose candidates for public office, seek to persuade public attitudes, and attempt to influence policy decisions of government.

LEARNING OBJECTIVES

1. Define and understand new terms and concepts introduced in the chapter.

2. Recognize and understand the involvement of political parties and interest groups in the American political process.

3. Identify and explain the functions of political parties.

4. Analyze the American two party system.

5. Describe types of minor parties in American politics.

6. Explain the structure of the Democratic and Republic parties.

LEARNING OBJECTIVES (cont.)

6. Recognize the declining status of political parties and assess the impact of this on the political process.

7. Evaluate criticisms of American political parties.

8. Distinguish between the activities of political parties and interest groups in the political process.

9. Define the term "interest group" and identify different types of interest groups.

10. Examine interest group activities in the political process and explain how important PAC's have become in politics.

11. Examine increased activities of interest groups in politics.

CHAPTER OUTLINE

I. Organized Political Groups
   A. Political parties
   B. Interest groups

II. Political Parties
   A. Definition
   B. Functions
      1. Nominating candidates for political office
      2. Educating the public
      3. Aggregating interests
      4. Simplify elections
      5. Serve as personnel agencies
      6. Organizing the decision making process
      7. Oppose the party in power

III. The American Two-Party system
   A. Traits
      1. Two parties
      2. Varied single-party dominance at times
   B. Reasons two parties dominate U. S. politics
      1. Institutionalized single member electoral system
      2. Cultural compromise theory
      3. Social consensus theory
   C. One-Party Areas
      1. Party loyalty historical legacy in South
      2. Citizen homogeneity favors one party
      3. Minority party unable to broaden base of support

CHAPTER OUTLINE (cont.)

    D. Nature of American Parties
        1. Parties are broad based coalition groups
        2. Parties avoid extreme positions
        3. Parties nominate moderate candidates
        4. Parties are highly decentralized
    E. Types of Minor Parties
        1. Ideological
        2. Single-issue
        3. Protest

IV. The Structure of Political Parties
    A. State organization
        1. State chairman
        2. State committee
        3. Congressional district
        4. County
        5. Town or city
        6. Ward
        7. Precinct
    B. National organization
        1. National chairman
        2. National committee
        3. National convention
    C. Decentralization of parties
        1. Parties have declined in importance
        2. Local parties extremely weak
    D. Decline of party identification
        1. Party loyalty has declined
        2. Independent voter identification has
            increased
        3. Realignment or dealignment
    E. Criticisms of American parties
        1. Voters have no clear choices
        2. Parties are too weak to control office holders

V. Interest Groups
    A. Definition
    B. Reasons for growth
        1. Federalism and separation of powers
        2. Greater specialization in society encourages
            growth
        3. Success encourages duplication
    C. Structure
        1. Most have charters and are organized
        2. Leaders exercise significant power

CHAPTER OUTLINE (cont.)

    D. Types
        1. Economic
            a. Agricultural
            b. Business and trade groups
            c. Labor
            d. Public employees
        2. Non-economic
            a. Racial
            b. Religious
            c. Gender
            d. Public interest
    E. New organizations
        1. Single-issue groups
        2. Political Actions Committees (PAC's)
    F. Interest group activities
        1. Electoral support and campaign expenditures
        2. Lobbying
            a. Congress
            b. Executive branch
        3. Litigation in courts
        4. Educational activities
            a. Influence public opinion
            b. Influence office holders
    G. Power of interest groups
        1. Larger groups exert power by membership
        2. Unified support and loyalty enhance power
        3. Congressional regulation: Regulation of Lobbying Act of 1946

VI. Conclusion
    A. Political parties in decline
    B. Growth and influence of interest groups
    C. Rise of single issue interest groups
    D. More people involved in politics
    E. Interest groups complicate, compromise, and accommodate
    F. Interest groups erode political accountability and responsibility

CHAPTER SUMMARY

Organized political activity in the United States is conducted primarily through two groups that influence public policy: political parties and interest groups.

Political parties are not mentioned in the Constitution but historically two major parties have monopolized our political process. However, there have been times when one party has been dominant.

34

CHAPTER SUMMARY (cont.)

The Democratic and Republican parties are coalition building parties that appeal to large blocks of diverse voters and are centrist in their political appeal. They also are very decentralized in structure and have been able to withstand challenges from minor parties that from time to time emerge but shortly disappear.

The structure of both major parties is similar and organized along the structure of our federal system of government. State political parties are loosely organized with the precinct level exercising campaign and organizational functions, while the county party exercises more influence in political and governmental matters.

In both major parties the national conventions nominate the presidential and vice presidential candidates and adopt party platforms but only meet every four years. The national committees and party national chairmen exercise influence over national party activities between conventions, but a president is the dominant figure in his party.

This century has witnessed the decline of powerful political parties, and in recent decades voters have increasingly shed party labels and voted across party lines. This trend has raised questions as to whether there is a "realignment" of party loyalties occurring or a "dealignment" of party identification among voters.

While decline in the American party system is taking place, interest groups are exerting greater influence in the political process. Interest groups have a narrower focus of political interest than political parties and can be categorized into economic and noneconomic interest. Recently, single issues interest groups have grown and since the early 1970's interest groups have created political action committees to channel significant sums of money into election campaigns. Other interest group activities include: manning election phone banks, distributing campaign literature, lobbying political officeholders, and filing lawsuits in the courts. Additionally, interest groups try to shape and direct public opinion in order to bring pressure on officeholders, and thus influence policy decisions.

Both political parties and interest groups represent organized efforts to influence government and public policy

CHAPTER SUMMARY(cont.)

but it appears as if political parties are in a stage of decline, while interest groups are becoming more powerful. This may be a mixed blessing as interest groups represent greater participation in the political process but such groups often lack the ability to bargain and compromise in providing solutions to problems of government.

PRACTICE EXERCISES

FILL IN THE BLANKS

1. _____ _____ for office is the main function of political parties.

2. _____ _____ do not run candidates for public office.

3. The lowest level of political party organization is the _____ organization.

4. The _____ _____ theory maintains that where there is fundamental agreement over the basic institutions of society a two party system dominates politics.

5. In the United States the _____ has had a one-party system which has dominated politics longer than any other region of the country.

6. The selection of a candidate for the presidential nomination is performed by the _____ _____.

7. The decline of political parties is referred to as _____.

8. The process of changing political parties is known as _____.

9. Interest groups like Mothers Against Drunk Driving (MADD) are known as _____ _____ interest groups.

10. In the _____ __ _____ ___ _____ _____ _____ case the Supreme Court declared segregation unconstitutional.

36

MULTIPLE CHOICE

11. Which one of the following is <u>not</u> a characteristic of
    American political parties?
    a. They avoid extremes
    b. They nominate moderate candidates
    c. They are decentralized
    d. They are highly disciplined

12. Which of the following political party organizations
    chooses the site of the national convention?
    a. National chairman
    b. National convention
    c. National committee
    d. State executive committee

13. Organizations created by interest groups to raise and
    spend campaign funds are:
    a. Trade associations
    b. Single issue groups
    c. Political action committees
    d. Ward committees

14. According to political scientist Walter Dean Burnham,
    American political parties appear to be losing their
    importance. This is called:
    a. Tradition
    b. Realignment
    c. Fragmentation
    d. Dealignment

15. Loyalty of voters toward a political party is called:
    a. Party realignment
    b. Party identification
    c. Party dealignment
    d. Party competition

16. The American political party system can be called:
    a. A one party system
    b. A two party system
    c. A three party system
    d. A four party system

17. Which one of the following party organizations is at
    the base of the political party structure?
    a. Ward
    b. Town committee
    c. Precinct
    d. State committee

MULTIPLE CHOICE (cont.)

18. There are several reasons why the number of interest groups has vastly increased in recent years. Which of the following is not a reason?
    a. Political parties now perform interest group functions
    b. Federalism and separation of powers
    c. Greater specialization in American society
    d. Success of some groups encourages other groups to form

19. Which of the following interest groups was organized to represent the "public interest"?
    1. Sierra Club
    2. Common Cause
    3. Urban League
    4. National Education Association

20. Among American voters, which of the following has occurred since the 1950's?
    a. The percentage of "independent" voters has risen
    b. The percentage of "strong partisan" voters has increased
    c. "Ticket splitting" has declined
    d. Voter participation has significantly increased

TRUE OR FALSE

21. There have been long periods of single party dominance in the American two-party system. _____

22. The national chairman of a political party is frequently at odds with the political party presidential nominee. _____

23. One by-product of the changes in the American party system is the increase of political party accountability. _____

24. Amicus curiae briefs are frequently used by interest groups to influence Congress. _____

25. The American political party system is often viewed as consisting of coalitions of various groups. _____

DISCUSSION, ESSAY

I. Identify and describe major functions of American political parties.

DISCUSSION, ESSAY (cont.)

II. Identify traits of the American party system, establish reasons why two parties dominate American politics, and explain characteristics of the two major political parties.

III. Examine the changing status of political parties in American politics and give reasons for the increase of independent voters and ticket-splitters.

IV. Distinguish between the activities of political parties and interest groups in the political process.

V. Explain how interest groups have changed in American politics and assess the increased importance of PAC's in politics.

6 NOMINATIONS AND ELECTIONS

CHAPTER OVERVIEW

Elections are the affirmation and renewal process of democracy. This chapter describes presidential nomination and election procedures, campaign strategies, election contests and the electoral college system. The chapter concludes with a brief overview of the Congressional election process and an assessment of changes in the current election system and the effects of these changes.

LEARNING OBJECTIVES

1. Define and understand terms and concepts introduced in the chapter on the electoral system.

2. Identify and explain nomination procedures used in the presidential election process.

3. Discuss the current presidential nomination procedures.

4. Understand public financing of the presidential campaign and distinguish between the present system of financing congressional campaigns.

5. Describe campaign strategies and explain the role of television in modern campaigns.

6. Examine the election system used in federal elections and explain the electoral college system.

7. Evaluate criticisms and reforms proposals for the electoral college system.

8. Understand and evaluate the congressional election system.

CHAPTER OUTLINE

I. Nomination Procedures
   A. Historical overview
      1. Caucus system
      2. Convention
      3. Primaries
         a. Single and run-off
         b. Closed
         c. Open
         d. Blanket
   B. Presidential nomination procedures
      1. Delegate selection
         a. Presidential primaries
         b. Caucuses and conventions
      2. National Convention
         a. Platform adoption
         b. Presidential candidate selection
         c. V. presidential candidate selection
      3. Reforms and criticisms
         a. Periodic reform
         b. National primary proposal
   C. Campaign financing
      1. Expensive costs and scandals
      2. Campaign finance reform
   D. Campaign strategies
   E. Television debates

II. The Election
   A. Registration
      1. Periodic
      2. Permanent
   B. Ballots
      1. Office column
      2. Party column

III. The Electoral College
   A. Operation
   B. Criticisms and reform

IV. Congressional Elections
   A. Competitiveness and incumbency
   B. Coattail effect
   C. Off year election

V. Conclusion
   A. Campaign Changes and Effects
   B. Criticisms

CHAPTER SUMMARY

The American nomination and election process for public office has gradually been reformed and democratized over the last two centuries. The legislative caucuses and mixed caucuses once used gave way to a convention and primary system that is used today. States basically control the election process with single and run-off primaries used in various states. Most states have closed election primaries while others use open primaries, and a few states have a blanket primary.

The American presidential nomination process combines a primary, caucus, and convention system that forces candidates seeking their party presidential nomination to have demonstrated some measure of popular voter support; the ability to gather delegates to the national convention; the ability to raise significant sums of money; and finally, to win the party nomination at the party national convention. Over a number of years the primary system has become more commonly used among the states and the national convention system has been reformed to make the conventions more representative of society. The Democratic Party has been more forceful in reform efforts but it has also created "superdelegates" so that elected Democratic officeholders may attend the party national convention.

The national conventions of each political party select presidential candidates, adopt party platforms, and permit the presidential candidates to choose their own vice presidential runningmates in preparation for the general election campaign.

The campaign begins shortly after the national conventions and have become extremely costly. Historically both political parties have received large financial donations from "fat cat" contributors and "media age" politics have made campaigns even more expensive. Illegal campaign donations and other campaign scandals led Congress to reform campaign financing in a series of Campaign Reform Acts of 1974, 1976, and 1979. The result of these reforms is that there exists public campaign funding in the presidential primaries, partial government funding of national conventions and public funding in the general election campaign. The laws also limits individual campaign donations and provides some regulation of PAC contributions. However, the laws do not provide public financing of congressional campaigns and congressional campaign costs have risen dramatically.

42

CHAPTER SUMMARY (cont.)

There are numerous criticisms of current campaign laws and these criticisms include allegations that the laws favor the two major parties and permit too much money in campaigns.

Issues and personalities influence campaign strategies as well as party registration and incumbency of office. Because Republicans are outnumbered by Democratic voter registration, Republican candidates rely more heavily on candidate identity and accomplishments. However, opponents will attack the record of an incumbent and today television and television debates have become more common in presidential campaigns. In close elections a positive candidate image projected by television may be the margin of victory.

The presidential campaign will also involve voter registration procedures and strategies as well as an electoral college victory strategy. Registration procedures may vary from state to state as well as ballot structure and these procedures and structure may be influential in determining how people vote. The electoral college system guarantees victory to a candidate who receives 270 electoral college votes and the "winner take all" system benefits large populous states so that a candidate can win by a plurality in possibly 12 states and get the Presidency. Indeed, the electoral college system has produced three presidents who have had fewer popular votes than their opponents but were elected by the electoral college. This system has been the subject of much criticism and many proposals for change, but the possibility for change appears remote unless the system fails.

Congressional elections are held more frequently than presidential elections due to the fact that all 435 House of Representative seats are elected each 2 years and one-third of the U.S.Senate seats become vacant at the same time. Increasingly House of Representative elections have become uncompetitive because of one-party election districts, incumbency, and gerrymandering which have worked to permit the Democrats to keep control of the House from 1955 to the present. Occasionally, a popular presidential candidate heading up an election ticket may influence results of congressional elections. 1980 is an example.

American elections historically have been lengthy but today they have become even longer and exceedingly complex. They are also more dependent on television and there are more primaries which require more money. Public financing has made possible greater opportunities for more candidates

43

CHAPTER SUMMARY (cont.)

to seek the Presidency but also has promoted the growth of PAC's and special interests and in turn weakened political parties. The present campaign and election system is heavily criticized but deep divisions exist as to the nature and direction of campaign and election reform.

PRACTICE EXERCISES

FILL IN THE BLANKS

1. In a _____ primary voters may choose a candidate from a different party for different offices on the same ballot.

2. Active political party members choosing delegates at a precinct meeting is an example of a political party _____.

3. The first state to use the presidential preference primary was _____.

4. The Democratic party in 1988 permitted Democratic governors, a number of Democratic members of Congress, members of the Democratic National Committee, and a few other selected officials to be delegates to the national convention. These officials were known as _____.

5. Generally the _____ party has outspent the _____ party in elections, but this latter party has received greater financial support from organized labor.

6. The _____ registration system permits a person to register and does not require reregistration unless the person moves or does not vote within a certain number of years.

7. Voting a _____ _____ means voting for all candidates of the same party on the ballot.

8. The drawing of congressional district boundaries to benefit the party in power is called _____.

9. Occupants for political office who run for re-election are known as _____.

PRACTICE EXERCISES (cont.)

10. A presidential campaign strategy for re-election that shows the President signing bills and "being presidential" is called a _____ _____ strategy.

MULTIPLE CHOICE

11. The political party primary that does not require a voter to register as a party member in order to vote in the party primary is known as:
    a. a closed primary
    b. an open primary
    c. a blanket primary
    d. a run-off primary

12. National party conventions perform a number of functions. Which is not a function of the national convention?
    a. to adopt a party platform
    b. to nominate a presidential candidate
    c. to nominate a vice presidential candidate
    d. to nominate members of a cabinet

13. Which of the following laws provide for public financing of presidential elections?
    a. the Federal Election Campaign Act of 1971
    b. the Political Activities Act of 1939
    c. the Corrupt Practices Act of 1925
    d. the Federal Election Campaign Act of 1974

14. Which one of the following methods of selection of candidates for public office was not developed until the twentieth century?
    a. the primary
    b. the legislative caucus
    c. the mixed caucus
    d. the convention

15. The most often used method of selecting delegates for presidential candidates today is:
    a. the caucus
    b. the convention
    c. the primary
    d. the general election

PRACTICE EXERCISES (cont.)

16. Which one of the following statements is <u>not</u> true of the electoral college system?
    a. all states have an equal number of electoral votes
    b. the winner-take-all popular vote system prevails
    c. large populous states dominate
    d. on occasion the popular vote winner has lost the election

17. A popular presidential candidate on the ballot may bring into office a number of members of his party. This is called:
    a. the surge effect
    b. the coattail effect
    c. the maintaining effect
    d. the reinstating effect

18. House officeholders enjoy a big advantage over challengers in elections. Which of the following is <u>not</u> an advantage?
    a. greater financial support
    b. gerrymandering
    c. the ability to send out mail free of charge
    d. little name recognition

19. Which of the following procedures was first used to nominate Andrew Jackson as President in 1832?
    a. the primary
    b. the legislative caucus
    c. the mixed caucus
    d. the convention

20. Vice presidential runningmates are customarily chosen:
    a. by open democratic election at the convention
    b. through primary election contests
    c. by convention ratification of a choice made by the presidential nominee
    d. with state caucus recommendation to the convention

TRUE OR FALSE

21. The open primary is used in most states for party nomination for office.   _____

22. The Republican party has made extensive reform of its rules to promote great participation of women and minorities in its convention.   _____

23. House of Representative elections have become less and less competitive.   _____

46

TRUE OR FALSE (cont.)

24. Wealthy campaign contributors are called "fat cats." _____

25. Most states use the office block ballot. _____

DISCUSSION, ESSAY

    I. Discuss the presidential nomination process, tracing the process from the primaries through the convention.

   II. Discuss public financing of presidential elections and distinguish it from the present system of financing congressional campaigns.

  III. Discuss the electoral college system and analyze proposals for reform of the system.

   IV. Explain various types of primary elections found among states.

    V. Discuss campaign strategies used in presidential elections.

7 CONGRESS

CHAPTER OVERVIEW

Chapter 7 of <u>American Democracy</u> introduces the study of governmental institutions. Congress was established by Article I of the United States Constitution and this chapter describes the functions of Congress, organizational structure, and the legislative process of Congress.

LEARNING OBJECTIVES

1. Identify, describe, and define basic terms and concepts necessary for an understanding of Congress.

2. Identify and describe the functions of Congress.

3. Examine, understand, and distinguish between the legislative and representational functions of Congress.

4. Recognize and explain the constitutionally assigned, non-lawmaking functions of Congress.

5. Explain the bases of congressional representation.

6. Examine the demographic characteristics of Congress and understand the responsibilities of state legislatures establishing congressional districts through reapportionment.

7. Describe the leadership of Congress and distinguish between institutional leadership and party leadership.

8. Examine and explain the committee system of Congress and understand the impact of the committee system in congressional operations.

9. Recognize the impact of Congressional reform and evaluate the impact of television on Congress.

LEARNING OBJECTIVES (cont.)

10. Understand the legislative process and distinguish between Senate and House of Representative legislative procedures.

CHAPTER OUTLINE

I. Introduction

II. Functions of Congress
   A. Legislative functions
      1. Taxing and spending
      2. Budget process
      3. Interstate commerce regulation
      4. Foreign affairs
      5. Implied powers
   B. Representation
   C. Other functions
      1. Oversight function
      2. Appointment confirmation
      3. Electoral functions
      4. Vice presidential disability functions
      5. Impeachment process
      6. Amendment responsibilities
      7. Disciplinary responsibilities

III. Congressional Districts
   A. State responsibilities
   B. Congressional reapportionment

IV. Two Houses of Congress
   A. Similarities
   B. Differences

V. Characteristics of Members
   A. Occupations/Professions
   B. Age
   C. Religion
   D. Gender and ethnicity

VI. Congressional Organization
   A. Institutional leaders
      1. Speaker of the House of Representatives
      2. President of the Senate
      3. President Pro-tempore of the Senate
   B. Party leaders
      1. House Majority Leader and assistants (whips)
      2. House Minority Leader and assistants (whips)
      3. Senate Majority Leader and assistants

CHAPTER OUTLINE (cont.)

      C. Committee system
         1. Types of committees
           a. Standing committees
           b. Select committees
           c. Joint committees
           d. Conference committees
         2. Committee assignments
         3. Committee chairmen
           a. powers
           b. selection and seniority
         4. Major committees
         5. Legislative bureaucracy
           a. employed congressional staff
           b. legislative staffing agencies

VII. Legislative Process
      A. Introduction of a bill
      B. Committee stage
      C. Legislative calendars
      D. Floor procedures
         1. House
         2. Senate
         3. Filibuster
         4. Television
      E. Voting
      F. Party influence and voting behavior
      G. Presidential actions

VIII. Conclusions
      A. Legislative process more open
      B. Television provides greater scrutiny of congressional activities

CHAPTER SUMMARY

Events of the 1780's led the framers of the Constitution to establish a Congress with significant powers to regulate national commerce and legislate directly on citizens. However, the framers also created a strong executive branch of government, an independent judiciary, and established two houses of Congress which all serve to temper increased congressional power and establish a balance among the different branches of government.

The functions of Congress may be summarized as legislative functions, representational functions, and other specific, constitutionally authorized functions. Legislative functions include the authority to raise taxes and spend revenue, control the budgetary process, regulate interstate

CHAPTER SUMMARY (cont.)

commerce, exercise authority in foreign and military affairs, ratify treaties, and exercise broadened authority all areas of its competence by the implied powers clause of in Article I of the Constitution.

Congress' representational functions involve a recognition that members are representatives of the districts which elect them to office and are thus expected to represent constituent interests. Representing constituent interests can be either by policymaking or providing services. Both of these may be important for re-election.

Other congressional functions include oversight functions of the executive branch, confirming presidential appointments, electoral functions, constitutional responsibilities in filling a vacancy in the Vice Presidency, and acting in presidential disability, impeachment, amending the Constitution, and finally, disciplining members of Congress.

The House of Representatives is a representative body that is constitutionally required to be reapportioned each ten years to reflect population shifts in society. Although the federal government performs the census and determines whether a state shall gain or lose representatives, state legislatures draw specific congressional district boundaries which are often "gerrymandered" according to which party has control of the state legislature. It is apparent that as a result of nationwide population shifts and reapportionment, the South and West will gain representation while the North will lose political influence in the House of Representatives.

A comparison of the Houses of Congress will show that there are similarities and that a number of differences exist in the two houses. Political parties control each house and the majority party in each house controls the committee system and the important leadership positions. However, the House is a much larger body than the Senate and has more formal procedures, complex rules, smaller election districts and two year terms. The Senate is smaller, permits unlimited debate, has six year terms, and statewide election districts.

Characteristics of members of Congress reveal that most members are upper middle class white males, over fifty, college educated, and Protestant, while women, blacks, and hispanics are underrepresented. Other data indicates that, by profession, most are lawyers followed by businessmen and those with a banking background.

CHAPTER SUMMARY (cont.)

Congressional leadership includes institutional leaders and party leaders. Institutional leaders are the Speaker of the House, the President of the Senate (Vice President of the United States), and the President Pro-tempore of the Senate. These are leaders of their respective institutions while the political parties select party leaders who provide partisan leadership on party and policy issues. Party leaders include majority leaders and whips in both houses and minority leaders and their whips.

The leadership system of Congress functions with the committee system in providing direction and continuity, but it is the committee system which performs the real work of Congress. Both houses have several types of committees that are very significant in congressional work. _Standing_ committees are specialized committees which are involved in the legislative process and hold hearings on legislation, while _select_ committees deal with specific issues but are not normally involved in the legislative process. Sometimes _joint_ committees of both houses will focus on significant issue areas but generally have no legislative functions. However, _conference_ committees are used often after each house completes as legislative issue and, with membership from each house, serve to iron out legislative differences between the House and Senate legislation. The _conference_ committee legislation is then adopted by the House and Senate and thus plays a significant role in the legislative process.

Committee chairmanship and committee assignments are made by the respective majority party organization in each house and reflect party control of each house. Chairmanship assignments have become more democratic in recent years and committee members have greater involvement in committee activities, while greater restraints have been placed on committee chairmen.

There are several major committees in the House and Senate that have an involvement in major policy issues of government. These committees in the Senate include the Appropriations Committee, the Foreign Relations Committee, the Finance Committee, the Armed Services Committee, and the Senate Budget Committee. Corresponding House major committees are the Rules Committee, the Ways and Means Committee, the Appropriations Committee, and the House Budget Committee.

The Congress employs thousands of people to assist the institution in performing its responsibilities. Members employ staff to assist them and committee staffs have also

CHAPTER SUMMARY (cont.)

grown in size. Congress has established additional research, monitoring, and investigative agencies that provide it with a wealth of information. Critics worry that far too often, staff assistants make government policy in the name of elected members of Congress.

Lawmaking in Congress is a process that involves several stages and begins long before the formal introduction of a legislative proposal. There are similarities between the legislative process in the Senate and the House of Representatives, but there are significant differences as well.

A bill can be introduced in either house and then is assigned to a standing committee for study and consideration. After passage by the committee, the bill (House and Senate procedures vary here) then is scheduled on a legislative calendar for floor action. Floor action involves discussion and debate and then the bill is voted on for final passage. Voting on issues may reflect political party considerations.

Once a bill has been passed by both houses in the same form, it goes to the President for his consideration. A President can sign a bill for it to become law or he can veto the bill, in which case Congress may attempt to override the veto by a two-thirds majority vote of each house.

In conclusion, the past twenty years have seen the greater democratization of the congressional system. Also the televising of congressional activities has opened the process to better scrutiny by constituents and permitted members to be more aware of issues before Congress. However, lobbyists have also become more sophisticated in pressuring Congress.

PRACTICE EXERCISES

FILL IN THE BLANKS

1. For an agency or department of government to spend money, an _____ bill establishes the policy program, and an _____ bill provides money to put into effect the policy or program.

2. In 1974 Congress adopted the _____ _____ _____ _____ _____ in an attempt to revitalize the budgetary process.

53

FILL IN THE BLANKS (cont.)

3. In 1985 Congress adopted the_____ _____ _____ _____ _____ _____ to cut federal spending and control the federal budget deficit.

4. Each ten years a federal census is taken to redistrict House of Representatives seats to adjust legislative districts to account for population shifts. This is known as _____.

5. The presiding officer of the United States Senate is formally known as the _____ ____ ____ _____.

6. Permanent legislative committees which hold hearings on bills and are part of the legislative process are known as _____ committees.

7. Committees with House and Senate members who try to establish compromises between House and Senate versions of the same bill are called _____ committees.

8. The _____ system provided that a House committee chairmanship would automatically go to the committee member from the majority party who had the greatest length of continuous service on that committee. This system was modified in 1973.

9. Non-public legislative bills are scheduled for debate on a _____ calendar.

10. On most legislative issues on the floor, the House will act as a _____ ____ _____ _____ and take action with a smaller number of members present.

MULTIPLE CHOICE

11. Congress has enacted legislation deregulating the trucking and airline industries. This legislative function of Congress relates to which of the following areas?
    a. budget adoption
    b. taxing and spending
    c. interstate commerce
    d. foreign affairs

12. Treaties are ratified by the Senate under which of the following provisions of the United States Constitution?
    a. Article I
    b. Article II
    c. Article III
    d. Article IV

MULTIPLE CHOICE   (cont.)

13. Should a Vice President vacate that office, a President nominates a successor. How would that vacancy be filled?
    a. Senate confirmation of the nominee
    b. House confirmation of the nominee
    c. Supreme Court confirmation of the nominee
    d. House and Senate confirmation of the nominee

14. Which of the following is not true of the Senate?
    a. It has more formal rules than the House
    b. It is smaller than the House
    c. It permits unlimited debate
    d. Its members have longer terms than House members

15. A presiding officer of the Senate, selected by the majority party to preside in the absence of the President of the Senate is:
    a. the majority leader
    b. the President Pro-tempore
    c. the committee chairman
    d. the Speaker

16. Committees of Congress which have both House and Senate membership and are used to study issues that may need action by Congress are known as:
    a. joint committees
    b. select committees
    c. standing committees
    d. temporary committees

17. Which of the following legislative calendars would be used for tax and appropriation measures?
    a. House calendar
    b. Private calendar
    c. Consent calendar
    d. Union calendar

18. Unlimited debate in the Senate may be ended by which of the following devices?
    a. consent calendar
    b. discharge petition
    c. closure vote
    d. senatorial courtesy

MULIPLE CHOICE (cont.)

19. Which of the following laws created the Congressional Budget Office to provide Congress with current information on the state of the nation's economy?
    a. Balanced Budget and Emergency Control Act of 1985
    b. Civil Rights Act of 1964
    c. Budget and Accounting Act of 1921
    d. Budget and Impoundment Control Act of 1974

20. Votes in the U.S. Senate are taken by a(n)
    a. Show of hands or standing votes
    b. Voice vote or roll call vote
    c. Electronic vote or teller vote
    d. Electronic vote or standing vote

TRUE OR FALSE

21. Television coverage of Congress is thought to permit members of Congress to keep abreast of issues. _____

22. A presidential veto may be overridden by three-fourths vote of both houses of Congress. _____

23. There is some belief that congressional staff aides may exercise significant influence over content of legislation and thus undermine elected members of Congress. _____

24. The power to declare war is a power granted to Congress under the Constitution. _____

25. The President may suspend members of Congress. _____

DISCUSSION, ESSAY

I. Identify and explain legislative functions of Congress.

II. Discuss the reasons for and effects of legislative reapportionment.

III. Compare and contrast similarities and differences between the House and Senate.

IV. Identify and describe the powers of the House and Senate leaders; distinguish between institutional leadership and party leadership.

V. Discuss the legislative process in Congress.

8 THE PRESIDENCY

CHAPTER OVERVIEW

The Presidency of the United States is not only one of the most significant institutions of government, it is also one of the most powerful positions in the world. The Constitution created this office in Article II. This chapter examines the qualifications for the office, roles and powers of the office, the limits and constraints on presidential power, and concludes with a discussion of the growth of the office.

LEARNING OBJECTIVES

1. Identify, describe, and define basic terms and concepts necessary for an understanding of the Presidency.

2. Understand the legal qualifications for the Presidency.

3. Recognize and comprehend issues of presidential succession, disability, and removal from office.

4. Identify and describe presidential roles and powers.

5. Identify and analyze limits on presidential power.

6. Examine the personal dimension of the Presidency and explain the importance of beliefs, motivations, and skills in using the powers of the office.

7. Examine the character analysis theory of presidential behavior and compare and contrast the four categories discussed.

8. Understand the constitutional foundation of the Vice Presidency and identify powers of that office.

9. Summarize reasons for the growth of presidential power.

CHAPTER OUTLINE

I. Selection and Removal
   A. Qualifications
   B. Succession
   C. Removal

II. Presidential Roles and Powers
   A. Chief of state
   B. Foreign policy maker
      1. Treaties, executive agreements
      2. Conduct of foreign policy
   C. Commander-in-chief
   D. World leader
   E. Chief administrator
   F. Chief legislator
      1. Sources of presidential involvement
      2. Presidential veto authority
      3. Presidential-congressional relations
   G. Party leader
   H. National opinion leader
   I. Economic manager

III. Limits on Presidential Power
   A. Judicial review
   B. Legislative veto
   C. War Powers Resolution
   D. Budget and Impoundment Control Act
   E. Media
   F. Bureaucracy
   G. Public opinion

IV. Personal Dimension
   A. Beliefs, motivations, skills
   B. Presidential character
      1. Active-positive
      2. Active-negative
      3. Passive-positive
      4. Passive-negative

V. The Vice President

VI. Conclusion

CHAPTER SUMMARY

The United States Constitution established the executive authority of government in a single executive: the President of the United States. The legal qualifications for President are stated in the Constitution and tradition has set political standards that reinforce the legal

CHAPTER SUMMARY (cont.)

qualifications. The questions of succession to that office and presidential disability are also found in Article II of the Constitution or the Twenty-fifth Amendment. Until the Twenty-fifth Amendment, there were no constitutional procedures for filling the Vice Presidency should that office become vacant and the Twenty-fifth Amendment also established procedures for temporarily vacating the Presidency because of disability.

The removal of a President is provided for by the Constitution through the impeachment process. The procedure is a two stage process that involves the House of Representatives voting articles of impeachment and the Senate convicting the President by two-thirds majority vote. Only President Andrew Johnson has been impeached, but he was not convicted by the Senate.

There are numerous roles that a President has in exercising powers of that office. Sources of these roles and powers are: the Constitution, laws of Congress, and precedents established by presidential action. Presidential roles include: chief of state, chief diplomat, commander-in-chief, world leader, chief administrator, chief legislator, party leader, national opinion leader, and economic leader.

Although the Presidency is one of the most powerful political officers in the world, there are limits on presidential power. These limits include restraints of a constitutional nature, laws adopted by Congress, and constraints that have emerged as society has developed and become more democratic. Examples of these limits are judicial review, the legislative veto, the War Powers Resolution, the Budget and Impoundment Control Act, the media, the bureaucracy of government, and public opinion.

There exists a personal dimension of the Presidency that is important in examining the office. The use of presidential power may be explained with the recognition that the personality and beliefs of the occupant may shape the use of presidential power. A very limited view of presidential power has led some Presidents to consciously establish limits on the use of their power, while other Presidents have taken a strong forceful view of presidential powers and used the office in a strongly persuasive manner to attain their goals. The persuasive skills of a President are basic to gaining popular and congressional support on policy goals. Recently there have been attempts to analyze and understand the relationship between character, personality,

CHAPTER SUMMARY (cont.)

politics and the Presidency. Dr. James David Barber has classified presidential character into four categories: active-positives, active-negatives, passive-positives, and passive-negatives. Barber's contribution to the study of the Presidency has been influential but also subject to criticism.

The Vice Presidency was created by the Constitution with the only constitutional responsibility of the Vice President being to preside over the Senate as President of the Senate. His only responsibilities are those which he may perform as a result of his relationship with the President. The Constitution provides that he is to succeed to the Presidency only upon presidential death, resignation, removal from office, or disability.

The modern Presidency is a Presidency of significant authority and power necessary to respond to problems in an industrial society, increased public expectations of presidential leadership, modern international crises, and the U.S. role as a superpower. Congress has sought to temper this power and scandals have weakened some aspects of presidential leadership, but one may conclude that the American Presidency is the dominant institution in government.

PRACTICE EXERCISES

FILL IN THE BLANKS

1. The Twenty-fifth Amendment was first used when Vice President _____ _____ resigned.

2. In the impeachment process articles of impeachment must be adopted by a _____ majority vote of the House of Representatives and the impeached official must be convicted by _____-_____ vote of the Senate to be removed from office.

3. A President may sign an _____ _____ in international affairs with a foreign head of state that has the same legal force as a treaty.

4. A President may refuse to sign a legislative bill and, if Congress adjourns within ten days, the bill fails to become law. This is known as a _____ _____.

FILL IN THE BLANKS (cont.)

5. According to Dr. James David Barber's analysis of presidential character, the _____-_____ type is ambitious and uses power in a struggle against a "hostile environment".

6. The _____-_____ presidential character dislikes conflict and stresses principles of duty and procedure.

7. A President's ceremonial duties fit into the role of _____ ____ _____.

8. Because a President's veto power is limited, members of Congress often attach unrelated legislative items to bills. Such legislative attachments are called _____.

9. A President campaigning on behalf of election of members of his party to office is carrying out the role of _____ _____.

10. In 1973, Congress passed legislation attempting to limit a President's war-making authority. This law is known as the _____ _____ _____.

MULTIPLE CHOICE

11. A President grants diplomatic recognition to foreign ambassadors. This illustrates his role as:
   a) chief of state
   b) foreign policy maker
   c) commander-in-chief
   d) world leader

12. A President is responsible for the management of agencies and departments of government. This responsibility illustrates his role as:
   a) world leader
   b) chief legislator
   c) party leader
   d) chief administrator

13. A President has significant responsibility for managing the economy. Congress by law established this responsibility for the President. The law which gave the President the authority to act was the:
   a. Budget and Accounting Act of 1921
   b. Budget and Impoundment Control Act of 1974
   c. Economic Opportunity Act of 1964
   d. Employment Act of 1946

MULTIPLE CHOICE (cont.)

14. According to Dr. James D. Barber's analysis of presidential character, which one of the following categories of presidential character should be avoided?
    a. active-positive
    b. active-negative
    c. passive-positive
    d. passive-negative

15. The only constitutional responsibility of the Vice President is:
    a. to veto bills passed by Congress
    b. to attend state funerals at presidential request
    c. to preside over the House as Speaker
    d. to preside over the Senate as President of the Senate

16. The War Powers Resolution of 1973:
    a. increased presidential war-making power
    b. requires congressional approval before using U.S. troops in combat
    c. gives the federal the legal power to interpret declarations of war
    d. attempts to place limits on a President's ability to use U.S. troops without congressional approval

17. The Twenty-fifth Amendment:
    a. permits the impeachment of the President
    b. provides for the Vice President to become acting President upon presidential disability
    c. provides for the resignation of the Vice President
    d. provides for the temporary rule of the country by executive order

18. In the impeachment trial of the President in the Senate:
    a. the Senate impeaches a President
    b. the Vice President presides over the trial
    c. the Chief Justice of the Supreme Court presides over the trial
    d. a simple majority vote convicts the President

19. The legislative veto:
    a. permits the courts to review executive authority
    b. permits Congress to veto specified presidential action
    c. requires the President to submit all executive actions to Congress
    d. has been held constitutional by the Supreme Court

MULTIPLE CHOICE (cont.)

20. Which of the following Presidents of the twentieth century was considered to be the first "strong" President?
    a) Theodore Roosevelt
    b) Franklin Roosevelt
    c) Harry Truman
    d) Lyndon Johnson

TRUE OR FALSE

21. Ronald Reagan is considered by James David Barber to be a passive-negative President. _____

22. The growth of presidential power is often regarded to be a result of action of strong Presidents. _____

23. Executive agreements between heads of state require Senate ratification. _____

24. The President has no item veto power. _____

25. Ronald Reagan is considered by James David Barber to be a passive-positive president. _____

DISCUSSION, ESSAY

  I. Identify and describe presidential roles.

 II. Discuss limits on presidential powers.

III. Discuss the concepts of "strong" and "weak" presidents. What are arguments for and against limits on presidential powers? Identify three Presidents in each category.

 IV. Discuss reasons for the growth of presidential powers.

  V. Examine the Twenty-fifth Amendment and discuss how this amendment attempts to deal with issues of presidential powers.

63

9 THE FEDERAL BUREAUCRACY

CHAPTER OVERVIEW

Government policies and programs are carried out by departments and agencies that constitute a governmental bureaucracy. This chapter explores the federal bureaucracy and issues associated with the bureaucracy. The organization of government is discussed as well as reasons given for the growth of bureaucratic power. The chapter describes restraints on government bureaucracy and concludes that governmental bureaucracy is the "fourth branch" of government.

LEARNING OBJECTIVES

1. Define and understand new terms and concepts related to the bureaucracy of government.

2. Understand Max Weber's concepts of authority and the bureaucracy and recognize the purpose of bureaucracy.

3. Analyze the structure of the federal bureaucracy.

4. List the agencies of the Executive Office of the President and understand how these agencies have increased their authority.

5. Recognize the background of the personnel of the bureaucracy and evaluate the significance of the civil service system.

6. Understand sources of bureaucratic power.

7. Analyze restraints on bureaucratic power.

CHAPTER OUTLINE

I. Bureaucracy
   A. Definition and purpose
   B. Types of authority
   C. Features

II. Executive Branch Organization
   A. Line agencies
      1. Departments
         a. State
         b. Treasury
         c. Defense
         d. Justice
         e. Interior
         f. Agriculture
         g. Commerce
         h. Labor
         i. Health and Human Services
         j. Housing and Urban Development
         k. Transportation
         l. Energy
         m. Education
         n. Veterans Affairs
      2. Sub-department organization
         a. Bureaus
         b. Field services
      3. Agencies
      4. Corporations
      5. Independent regulatory commissions
      6. Independent control and service agencies
   B. Staff agencies
      1. Cabinet
      2. Executive Office
         a. White House Office
         b. Office of Management and Budget
         c. Council of Economic Advisors
         d. National Security Council
         e. Other offices

III. Federal Bureaucrats
   A. Size of the bureaucracy
   B. Professions/occupations
   C. Spoils system
   D. Civil service
      1. Merit
      2. Classification
      3. Civil service reform
   E. Political Executives

CHAPTER OUTLINE (cont.)

IV. Sources of Bureaucratic Power
    A. Expertise
    B. "Iron triangle" influence
    C. Delegation of congressional power

V. Restraints on Bureaucracy
    A. Presidential powers
        1. Appointive powers
        2. Removal powers
        3. Reorganizational powers
        4. Presidential leadership
    B. Congressional powers
        1. Budgetary powers
        2. Organizational powers
        3. Lawmaking powers
            a. Freedom of Information Act of 1966
            b. Budget and Impoundment Control Act of 1974
        4. Legislative oversight
    C. Judicial review
    D. Other restraints
        1. Media exposure
        2. Interest group pressures
        3. Bureaucratic internal competition
        4. Bureaucratic values
        5. Deregulation

VI. Conclusions
    A. Bureaucracy is large and powerful
    B. Bureaucracy is a convenient political scapegoat

CHAPTER SUMMARY

Programs and policies established by Congress and the President are carried out by a vast federal bureaucracy that has been established in over two hundred years of government. Modern bureaucracy is based on a "rational-legal authority" model as identified by Max Weber rather than "traditional authority" or "charismatic authority" models. Features of an ideal bureaucracy are reflected in present governmental bureaucracy although there exists failings which are characteristic of human behavior.

The executive branch of the United States Government is loosely organized into line agencies, which are to carry out policies of government and provide services of government, and staff agencies which are to provide services and information to the federal executive.

Line agencies include the fourteen Cabinet departments, federal agencies, governmental corporations, independent

CHAPTER SUMMARY (cont.)

regulatory commissions, and service and control agencies which provide personnel and supplies for agencies and maintain federal facilities. Each unit of organization has an internal structure and hierarchy and the vast majority of its personnel residing outside the nation's capital.

Staff agencies include the Cabinet and the Executive Office of the President. This level of the bureaucracy advises the President on issues and policy matters and also Cabinet members head up departments which carry out policies of government. The Executive Office includes the White House Office, the Office of Management and Budget, the Council of Economic Advisors, and the National Security Council. The offices in the Executive Office have increased in in policymaking while the influence of the Cabinet has has declined.

The size of the federal bureaucracy has grown significantly but has stabilized at around 3 million people. The bureaucrats today are highly specialized by profession and occupation and can be found around the world. They are employed using a civil service merit system based on standardized examinations and placed on a classification scale based on job title, duties, and job qualifications. This classification scale also contains wage and salary scales and is a reform of the spoils system of the nineteenth century. However, the top level of the bureaucracy consists of political appointees who implement the policies of the President and require confirmation by the Senate.

The bureaucracy is very powerful and has several sources of power and influence. Its immense size is one source of power and its specialized knowledge gives it enormous influence in dealing with Congress and top administrative officials. Another source of bureaucratic power is the "iron triangle" relationship between the bureaucratic agency, appropriate congressional committee, and the interest group that interacts with the appropriate congressional committee and the bureaucracy. Also Congress has enacted broad policy goals and left detailed policy implementation to agencies of government that are to flesh out policy goals. The effect of this has been to enhance bureaucratic influence in policymaking.

There are many restraints on governmental bureaucracy and these restraints range from presidential powers to

CHAPTER SUMMARY (cont.)

congressional powers and other restraints as media exposure and private influences on policymaking. Also inter-agency competition may serve to restrain bureaucratic growth and recent government emphasis on deregulation has served to establish limits on bureaucratic growth.

One must realize that the governmental bureaucracy is large and that bureaucratic decisions affect the daily lives of millions of Americans. However, it should be noted that governmental bureaucracy may frustrate citizen interest in government and that the bureaucracy serves as a political scapegoat for unpopular policies of government.

PRACTICE EXERCISES

FILL IN THE BLANKS

1. Unquestioned authority which is based on authority that is passed from generation to generation is called _____ authority.

2. Authority based on personal qualities of a leader is called _____ authority.

3. Agencies which carry out government policies and provide services are called _____ agencies.

4. Executive departments are divided into _____ which are headed by chiefs.

5. The Federal Deposit Insurance Corporation is an example of a government _____.

6. Agencies such as the Council of Economic Advisors, the White House Office, and the National Security Council are to provide staff assistance to the President. This office is called the _____ _____ _____ _____ _____.

7. The _____ system permitted Presidents to appoint friends and supporters to bureaucratic office.

8. Political appointees nominated by the President to head policymaking positions in the bureaucracy must be confirmed by the _____.

9. Significant power relationships between a government agency, a congressional committee, and a special interest group are called an _____ _____.

68

FILL IN THE BLANKS (cont.)

10. Congressional power to review bureaucratic agency actions and thus exercise control over the executive is called congressional _____.

MULTIPLE CHOICE

11. Authority which is based on the personal qualities of a leader as Mahatma Gandhi or Adolf Hitler is called:
    a. traditional authority
    b. rational-legal authority
    c. dictatorial authority
    d. charismatic authority

12. Which of the following laws were not written to exercise control over the executive branch of government:
    a. Civil Rights Act of 1964
    b. Budget and Accounting Act of 1921
    c. Freedom of Information Act of 1966
    d. Budget and Impoundment Control Act of 1974

13. In which of the following laws did Congress give control over the budget process to the executive branch?
    a. Civil Rights Act of 1964
    b. Budget and Accounting Act of 1921
    c. Freedom of Information Act of 1966
    d. Budget and Impoundment Control Act of 1974

14. Which of the following offices is not found within the Executive Office of the President?
    a. Office of Management and Budget
    b. National Security Council
    c. White House Office
    d. Department of Transportation

15. A theory of bureaucracy that strongly influenced the shaping of modern bureaucracy was developed by the sociologist:
    a. Karl Marx
    b. Max Weber
    c. Robert Dahl
    d. Sam Moore Walton

16. Agencies which gather information and provide services to other agencies are called:
    a. Departments
    b. Line Agencies
    c. Staff agencies
    d. Commissions

MULTIPLE CHOICE (cont.)

17. A commission which investigates violations of anti-trust law and looks into deceptive labeling is the:
    a. Federal Trade Commission
    b. Interstate Commerce Commission
    c. Securities and Exchange Commission
    d. Federal Election Commission

18. Which of the following entities is responsible for reviewing government budgets and legislative proposals with the President?
    a. U.S. Treasury Department
    b. Internal Revenue Service
    c. General Accounting Office
    d. Office of Management and Budget

19. Which of the following is regarded as a source of bureaucratic power?
    a. Presidential removal power
    b. Impoundment legislation
    c. Expertise
    d. Judicial review

20. Which of the following offices are regarded by Thomas Cronin as part of the "inner" Cabinet?
    a. Secretaries of Labor, Agriculture, Health and Human Services
    b. T.V.A., F.C.C., and N.R.C.
    c. Secretaries of State, Defense, Treasury, and Attorney General
    d. C.A.B, U.S. Postal Service, and F.T.C.

TRUE OR FALSE

21. Independent commissions were created by the Constitution. _____

22. Newspapers cannot be considered as able to exercise restraints on governmental bureaucracy. _____

23. Government bureaucrats serve all over the globe and may include lawyers, cooks, and people from all walks of life. _____

24. Congress has increased bureaucratic power by delegation of authority to agencies and departments to make rules. _____

25. The Freedom of Information Act of 1966 was considered to have significantly increased bureaucratic power. _____

70

DISCUSSION, ESSAY

   I. Discuss sources of power of the federal bureaucracy.

  II. Identify the main features of an ideal bureaucracy.

 III. Explain how the executive branch is organized.

  IV. Briefly identify and describe the offices which are found in the Executive Office of the President.

   V. Discuss restraints on the federal bureaucracy.

10 THE JUDICIARY

CHAPTER OVERVIEW

The American legal and judicial system is described in this chapter. Topics encompassed are the types of law found in the United States, an overview of court proceedings, a description of the dual state-federal court system, and an in-depth examination of U.S. Supreme Court procedures. Also, this chapter reviews the procedures for appointment to the federal judiciary, describes the functions of the federal judiciary, and raises such controversial issues as judicial restraint, judicial activism, and the debate over the doctrine of "original intent".

LEARNING OBJECTIVES

1. Define and understand new concepts related to the judiciary.

2. Explain major types of law in the United States.

3. Recognize the following aspects of the legal and judicial system: the adversary system, the functions of courts, the role of the judge, court jurisdiction, and the structure of state and federal courts.

4. Identify and explain the organization of the federal judiciary.

5. Explain the operations of the U. S. Supreme Court.

6. Describe the selection process of federal judges.

7. Understand the functions of the judiciary and recognize restrictions placed on the federal court system.

LEARNING OBJECTIVES (cont.)

8. Contrast the concepts of judicial restraint and judicial activism.

9. Assess the doctrine of "original intent."

CHAPTER OUTLINE

I. The Law
   A. Types
      1. Common Law
      2. Equity
      3. Statutory law
      4. Constitutional law
      5. Administrative law
   B. Civil and Criminal Law
      1. Criminal law
         a. Plaintiff
         b. Defendant
         c. Misdemeanors
         d. felonies
      2. Civil law

II. The Adversary System
   A. Courts
   B. Judges

III. The Dual Court System
   A. Jurisdiction over cases
   B. State courts
   C. Federal courts
      1. Constitutional courts
      2. Legislative courts
   D. U. S. District Courts
   E. U. S. Court of Appeal

IV. The U. S. Supreme Court
   A. Oral arguments
   B. Conference
   C. Opinions
      1. Majority
      2. Concurring
      3. Dissenting
   D. The Chief Justice
   E. Access to the Supreme Court
      1. Appeal
      2. Certiorari

CHAPTER OUTLINE (cont.)

    V.   Selection of Federal Judges
         A.   Lower Federal Court judges
         B.   U. S. Supreme Court appointments

   VI.   Functions of the Judiciary
         A.   Judicial review
              1.   Origins: Marbury v. Madison (1803)
              2.   History
         B.   Restrictions on the courts
              1.   Impeachment
              2.   Laws of Congress
              3.   Public acceptance of decisions

  VII.   Constitutional Interpretation
         A.   Judicial restraint
         B.   Judicial activism
         C.   Original intent

 VIII.   Conclusion

SUMMARY

The American legal and judicial system functions to hear and
resolve legal disputes that arise in the court system.
Several types of law are used in the American court system
and include common law, equity, statutory law,
constitutional law, and administrative law. Both common law
and equity developed in England and further evolved in the
colonies and play an important function in our legal and
judicial system.

There are two broad areas of law in the United States:
civil law and criminal law. Criminal law regulates conduct
and behavior in society and is enforced by government.
Punishment for criminal law violations include prison or
jail, fines, and even the death penalty, depending on
whether the criminal violations are minor (misdemeanors) or
serious (felonies). Civil law usually involves contract
disputes and private rights enforceable in a court of law.

The American legal and judicial system is established on an
adversary basis by which the courts are authorized by the
Constitution to resolve legal disputes. Judges preside over
the courts, control the proceedings, and pronounce
sentences, although juries may be involved in the
proceedings and pronounce verdicts.

CHAPTER SUMMARY (cont.)

All states and the federal government have their own legal and judicial systems, with state legal and judicial systems varying from state to state.

Federal courts are created under the Constitution as constitutional courts (Article III) or legislative courts (Article I). Article III courts have their jurisdiction specified by the constitution and some possess original jurisdiction while others hear cases only on appeal. The U. S. Supreme Court possesses both original and appellate jurisdiction. All federal constitutional court judges are appointed by the President and confirmed by the U. S. Senate for a term of good behavior.

The lowest level of federal constitutional courts are the United States districts courts which hear both civil and criminal cases, hold trials, and possess only original jurisdiction. The next highest level courts are the thirteen United States Courts of appeal which have only appellate jurisdiction and usually hear cases as three judge panels.

The United States Supreme Court heads up the federal judiciary and hears cases from October through June of each year. Most cases reach the Supreme Court by either appeal or through certiorari. There are several stages in cases that are heard by the U. S. Supreme Court and these stages include: presenting legal briefs to the Court, oral arguments made before the Court, judicial conferences where justices decide the case, and writing the majority, concurring, and dissenting opinions. The Chief Justice presides over the Supreme Court, may assign opinions to be written, as well as make a presentation to the Friday Court conferences. Thus his influence may be significant.

Since Federal judges are chosen by the President, politics often plays a large role in the appointment and confirmation process. Lower federal judges are selected in a procedure that reflects "senatorial courtesy" and Supreme Court appointees undergo a scrutiny that at times may become contentious. A few nominees have been refused confirmation by the Senate and occasionally Congress has also impeached and removed federal judges from office.

The federal judiciary functions to resolve legal disputes, interpret statutes, review executive actions, and interpret the Constitution. Occasionally, the judiciary may assert its power of judicial review to strike down laws and executive actions which it determines are unconstitutional. The power of judicial review was assumed by the Supreme Court in

75

CHAPTER SUMMARY (cont.)

the Marbury v. Madison case of 1803.

Although the judiciary is very powerful, its authority can be restricted. Congress can change the jurisdiction of the courts and write legislation affecting the judiciary and may impeach and remove judges from office. Finally, public willingness to accept court decisions may hamper enforcement of court decisions.

Great controversy exists over the proper role of the federal courts in policymaking. An argument of judicial self-restraint holds that judges are to interpret law and let elected officials make policy. A counter-argument of judicial activism maintains that courts should act to establish policy of government. Recently a new controversy has emerged as some have suggested that the judiciary should interpret the Constitution consistent with the "original intent" of the framers who wrote the document. Opponents of this view argue that such an interpretation would not permit social change or permit the Constitution to be adapted to changing conditions in society.

In conclusion, one could state that the judiciary and specifically the U. S. Supreme Court, play an important role in protecting rights of citizens, especially from arbitrary and illegal government actions.

PRACTICE EXERCISES

FILL IN THE BLANKS

1. Under the doctrine of _____ _____ the Constitution should be interpreted as the framers had written the document.

2. Under the doctrine of _____ _____, judges may interpret their authority to declare laws unconstitutional and set policy direction themselves.

3. Executive agencies may write rules which have the effect of law. This is called _____ _____.

4. The body of law which regulates private rights and contract rights among private individuals is called _____ law.

5. Under the _____ system one party files a court suit against another person and the court acts as an umpire.

FILL IN THE BLANKS (cont.)

6. Legislative written law is called _____ _____.

7. _____ is the term used to describe the right of a court to hear a case.

8. Courts which are created by Congress under Article I of the Constitution are _____ courts.

9. Minor criminal offenses are called _____.

10. _____ opinions are written by judges who agree with a majority in a court decision but reach their legal conclusion for different reasons.

MULTIPLE CHOICE

11. A body of law that developed by judges decisions rendered in court cases is called:
    a. equity
    b. statutory law
    c. constitutional law
    d. common law

12. Court interpretation of state or federal constitutions is called:
    a. equity
    b. statutory law
    c. constitutional law
    d. common law

13. For a judge to defer to elective branches of government and not make policy by judicial decision is called:
    a. original intent
    b. judicial restraint
    c. judicial activism
    d. judicial decree

14. In which of the following court cases did the Supreme Court assert the doctrine of judicial review?
    a. Muskrat v. United States
    b. Marbury v. Madison
    c. Brown v. Board of Education of Topeka
    d. Buckley v. Valeo

15. The body of law which provides punishment for acts that endanger public welfare is:
    a. administrative law
    b. equity
    c. criminal law
    d. civil law

77

MULTIPLE CHOICE (cont.)

16. A court which hears a case for the first time is said
    to possess:
    a. original jurisdiction
    b. statutory authority
    c. appellate jurisdiction
    d. concurrent jurisdiction

17. The party who brings a case to court is referred to
    as:
    a. the defendant
    b. the respondent
    c. the plaintiff
    d. the judge

18. Judges appointed to constitutional courts and confirmed
    by the Senate serve:
    a. for a term of ten years
    b. for a term of twenty years
    c. for a term of good behavior
    d. for a term of twenty-five years

19. Which of the following courts is an example of a
    legislative court:
    a. the U.S. Supreme Court
    b. the U.S. Court of Military Appeals
    c. the U.S. Circuit Court of Appeals
    d. the U.S. District Court

20. Written arguments presented in a court case are called
    a. majority opinions
    b. a writ of certiorari
    c. the plaintiff
    d. a brief

TRUE OR FALSE

21. The U.S. Supreme Court is the only court actually
    created by the U.S. Constitution.   _____

22. The most common means for a case to reach the U.S.
    Supreme Court is by appeal.   _____

23. Perhaps one of the most important functions of the U.S.
    Supreme Court in recent decades has been to exercise
    original jurisdiction.   _____

24. Legislative court judges are appointed for a fixed
    number of years.   _____

TRUE OR FALSE (cont.)

25. Constitutional courts are created under Article I of the Constitution. _____

DISCUSSION, ESSAY

I. Identify and explain five types of law found in the United State.

II. Discuss the concepts of civil and criminal law.

III. Discuss the structure and jurisdiction of the federal constitutional court system.

IV. Discuss the legal and judicial responsibilities of the U.S. Supreme Court and describe the procedures by which cases are resolved in the Supreme Court.

V. Discuss the functions of the federal judiciary and evaluate the concepts of judicial restraint and judicial activism as they relate to these functions.

11 CIVIL LIBERTIES

CHAPTER OVERVIEW

Chapter 11 discusses and analyzes civil liberties in American society. The basic Constitution contains some protection of civil liberties and the Bill of Rights vastly enhances citizen protection against the arbitrary use of governmental power.

The Bill of Rights was extended to protect citizens against state governments by Supreme Court interpretation and not all of the amendments of the Bill of Rights apply as restraints to state action. Liberties developed and examined in this chapter are: religious freedom, speech, assembly, right to petition, and the rights of criminally accused individuals.

LEARNING OBJECTIVES

1. Define and understand new terms and concepts relating to civil liberties.

2. Distinguish between civil liberties and civil rights.

3. Explain the process of applying the Bill of Rights to states.

4. Discuss the freedom of religion guarantees in the Bill of Rights.

5. Analyze constitutional protections of free speech, freedom of the press, freedom of assembly, and the right to petition government.

6. Examine constitutional protections of the rights of the criminally accused.

CHAPTER OUTLINE

I. Bill of Rights
   A. Civil liberties
   B. Civil rights
   C. Extension to states

II. Freedom of Religion
   A. Free Exercise
   B. Establishment clause
      1. Aid to religious schools
      2. School prayer

III. Freedom of Speech, Press, Assembly, Petition
   A. Prior Restraint
   B. Sedition activities
   C. The First Amendment and public places
      1. Assembly
      2. Speech
      3. Petition
   D. Right of association
   E. Freedom of the press
   F. Obscenity
   G. Libel and slander
   H. Commercial speech
   I. Symbolic speech
   J. Press freedom v. fair trial
   K. Protection of private property

IV. Rights of the Criminally Accused
   A. Ex post facto laws
   B. Bills of attainder
   C. Search and seizure
      1. Search warrants and warrantless searches
      2. Exclusionary rule
      3. Electronic surveillance
   D. Freedom from self-incrimination
   E. Indictment by Grand Jury
   F. Protection against double jeopardy
   G. Right to legal counsel
   H. Confessions
      1. Miranda v. Arizona
      2. Exceptions
   I. Eighth Amendment
      1. Excessive bail
      2. Cruel and unusual punishment
      3. Death penalty
      4. Plea bargaining

V. Conclusion

CHAPTER SUMMARY

The American constitutional system contains a number of protections for citizens against arbitrary rule by government. These guarantees take the from of civil liberties which are the individual rights that are guaranteed in the Constitution. Many of these guarantees are found in the Bill of Rights, which the U, S. Supreme court interpreted as applying a restraint on state government through the due process clause of the Fourteenth Amendment of the U. S. Constitution.

There are two clauses of the First Amendment which guarantee religious freedom. The free exercise clause guarantees freedom of religious belief and practice, but the courts have held that government may regulate certain religious practices. The establishment clause guarantees religious freedom from establishment of religion by law and most court interpretations limit governmental aid to religious schools, except in narrowly defined areas. Generally, such aid must: have a specific secular purpose, neither promote nor inhibit religious instruction, avoid excessive government involvement with religion, and is more likely to be constitutional if it is pupil-benefit-related rather than institutionally related. The establishment clause also is interpreted as prohibiting required or voluntary religious activities in public schools if these activities are part of a school sponsored program.

There are other major freedoms and liberties guaranteed in the Bill of Rights and these guarantees include freedom of the press which prevents government from exercising prior restraint in issues involving the press. However, commercial speech as well as materials deemed obscene or pornographic may be subjected to governmental regulation. Also reporters may be subject to giving court testimony in libel cases and criminal investigations.

Other guarantees protecting citizens are freedom of speech, assembly, the right to petition government, and private property rights. Speech is strongly protected even to the point that advocacy of rebellion is a form of protected speech unless violence is imminent and the speech is likely to produce violence. Less volatile speech and assembly is also protected in public places, but the Supreme Court has upheld laws regulating time, place, and manner of public assembly or demonstrations. There are other guarantees as freedom of association, a degree of protection of symbolic speech, and the Fifth Amendment guarantees property owners just compensation if government takes private property for public purposes.

CHAPTER SUMMARY (cont.)

The Constitution   Bill of Rights contains protections for the rights of the criminally accused. **Ex post facto** laws and bills of attainder are prohibited and police search and seizure authority under the Fourth Amendment is constrained. The exclusionary rule and requirements for legal warrants for electronic surveillance both protect the criminally accused.

The Fifth Amendment contains protection of citizens from self-incrimination and double jeopardy in criminal cases, while the Sixth Amendment guarantees a right to legal counsel and requires criminal suspects to be advised of their legal rights (Miranda v. Arizona). The Eighth Amendment provides that excessive bail shall not be required and that cruel and unusual punishment is prohibited. However, the death penalty is permitted, and in fact many criminal cases result in numerous suspects pleading guilty to lesser charges.

The U. S. constitutional system places great emphasis on rights and liberties for citizens. The Supreme Court is an institution of government that protects these rights and liberties while serving to impose restraints on other governmental institutions.

PRACTICE EXERCISES

FILL IN THE BLANKS

1. The _____ _____ of the First Amendment prohibits numerous types of state and church associations.

2. The U. S. Supreme Court has generally rejected _____ _____ or censorship as a means of restricting freedom of the press.

3. _____ is defined as incitement to rebellion.

4. In the _____ __ _____ case of 1973, the U. S. Supreme Court tried to establish certain tests to determine whether a work was obscene.

5. Wearing an armband is a form of _____ speech.

6. A _____ ___ _____ is legislative punishment without benefit of judicial trial.

FILL IN THE BLANKS (cont.)

7. The _____ Amendment to the Constitution places restraints on police authority to engage in search and seizure in criminal cases.

8. In the 1961 case _____ __ _____ the Supreme Court prohibited evidence that was illegally seized.

9. In the _____ __ _____ case of 1967, the Supreme Court threw out wiretaps as a violation of search and seizure protection of the Constitution.

10. A jury which returns and indictment is the _____ jury.

MULTIPLE CHOICE

11. To be <u>forced</u> to give testimony against oneself is called:
    a. double jeopardy
    b. bill of information
    c. symbolic speech
    d. self incrimination

12. The right to legal counsel is protected under the following constitutional amendment:
    a. First
    b. Sixth
    c. Fourth
    d. Fifth

13. In 1966, the U. S. Supreme Court ruled that a suspect must be advised of his constitutional rights after he was taken into custody or "significantly deprived of freedom of action." The court case was:
    a. Powell v. Alabama
    b. Brown v. Board of Education of Topeka
    c. Miranda v. Arizona
    d. Gideon v. Wainwright

14. Often a government prosecutor will drop a serious charge against a criminal defendant if the accused will agree to a guilty charge on a lesser criminal offense. This is called:
    a. Cruel and unusual punishment
    b. Excessive bail
    c. Self incrimination
    d. Plea bargaining

MULTIPLE CHOICE (cont.)

15. The constitutional amendment which has been interpreted as permitting some of the protections of the Bill of Rights to be applied as restraints on state action is the:
   a. Thirteenth Amendment
   b. Fourteenth Amendment
   c. Fifteenth Amendment
   d. Sixteenth Amendment

16. Aid to parochial schools is considered under which one of the following clauses of the First Amendment?
   a. The establishment clause
   b. The free exercise clause
   c. The freedom of assembly clause
   d. The freedom of the press clause

17. In 1962 the Supreme Court held that required, non-denominational prayer in public schools was a violation of the establishment clause of the First Amendment. The case was:
   a. Miller v. California
   b. Engel v. Vitale
   c. Torasco v. Walkins
   d. Reynolds v. United States

18. The constitutional amendment which guarantees a right to a "fair trial" before an "impartial jury" is the:
   a. First Amendment
   b. Fourth Amendment
   c. Fifth Amendment
   d. Sixth Amendment

19. Government may take private property for public use by using procedures of:
   a. The Fifth Amendment
   b. The Sixth Amendment
   c. The Seventh Amendment
   d. The Ninth Amendment

20. In 1963, the right to legal counsel was applied to all "state felony trials" in which of the following cases?
   a. Powell v. Alabama
   b. Brown v. Board of Education of Topeka
   c. Miranda v. Arizona
   d. Gideon v. Wainwright

TRUE OR FALSE

21. The Bill of Rights has always been applied as limits to state government action. _____

22. Voluntary prayers are permitted in public schools as a part of a school sponsored program. _____

23. There is some protection of freedom of association under the First Amendment. _____

24. Reporters' notes may be subpoenaed in criminal investigation. _____

25. Commercial speech may be regulated if it is false or misleading. _____

DISCUSSION, ESSAY

I. Discuss the religious guarantees of the First Amendment.

II. Discuss the rights of the criminally accused under the Fourth, Fifth and Sixth Amendments.

III. Discuss protections of the Eighth Amendment.

IV. Discuss press protections of the First Amendment as these protections relate to reporters, newspapers, obscenity, libel and slander.

V. Discuss conflicts between press freedom and Sixth Amendment protection of a right to a fair trial. What means have been used to minimize such conflicts?

12 CIVIL RIGHTS

CHAPTER OVERVIEW

The struggle of minorities and women in American society to enjoy equal rights and end discrimination based on race, national origin, and sex has been one of great length. This struggle involves constitutional amendments, legislation passed by Congress, and Supreme Court interpretation of constitutionally protected rights. There has been great progress made in recent decades of the Twentieth Century and yet significant controversy remains.

LEARNING OBJECTIVES

1. Define and understand new terms and concepts introduced in the chapter on civil rights.

2. Understand the history of the struggle over slavery.

3. Describe the efforts during Reconstruction to assimilate blacks into American society.

4. Explain the constitutional and legal foundations of segregation.

5. Recognize the constitutional and legal results of the civil rights struggle.

6. Evaluate the arguments for and against affirmative action.

7. Understand the struggle of women for equal rights in American society.

8. Comprehend the Supreme Court tests to determine whether different treatment of citizens under the equal protection clause of the Fourteenth Amendment is legal or illegal.

LEARNING OBJECTIVES (cont.)

9. Assess the significance of the Roe v. Wade decision of Supreme Court in relation to the struggle for women's rights.

CHAPTER OUTLINE

I. Historic Struggle of Non-White Americans
   A. Struggle over slavery, and aftermath
      1. Missouri Compromise
      2. Dred Scott decision
      3. Emancipation Proclamation of 1863
      4. Thirteenth Amendment
      5. Fourteenth Amendment
      6. Fifteenth Amendment
      7. Civil rights laws of 1860's and 1870's
   B. Legal segregation and discrimination
      1. Plessy v. Ferguson
         a. Separate but equal doctrine
      2. Grandfather clauses
      3. White primary
      4. Poll taxes
      5. Literacy tests

II. The Establishment of Equal Rights
   A. Laws and court decisions
      1. Voting Rights Acts of 1965,1970,1975,1982
      2. Brown v. Board of Education
         a. de jure segregation
         b. de facto segregation
      3. Civil Rights Act of 1964
         a. Public accommodations
         b. Non-discrimination in employment
         c. Non-discrimination by gender
      4. Effects of demonstrations, marches, sit-ins
   B. Promoting equal opportunity and equal access
      1. Affirmative action
         a. Active recruitment
         b. Quotas, ratios
      2. Controversy over affirmative action
         a. Advantages
         b. Disadvantages
         c. Regents of University of California v. Baake
   C. Women's rights
      1. Struggle
      2. Agenda
      3. Legislation to end discrimination
         a. Civil Rights Act of 1964
         b. Equal Employment Opportunity Act of 1972
         c. Education Amendment of 1972

CHAPTER OUTLINE (cont.)

4. Constitutional law interpretation
   a. Roe v. Wade
   b. Substantiality constitutional test

CHAPTER SUMMARY

This chapter details a lengthy struggle to extend civil rights to all citizens and end discrimination based on race, creed, color, and sex. This struggle has challenged the democratic principle of equalities stated in the Declaration of Independence beginning with the institution of slavery which was established in the colonies and institutionalized in the Constitution.

In the first few decades of the Constitution, conflict arose over extending slavery to new territories entering the Union. Political compromises and court decisions delayed the decisive struggle over slavery until the 1860's and the Civil War.

The Civil War brought about an end to slavery, first through the Emancipation Proclamation, and then in the war's aftermath with the Thirteenth Amendment. Later the Fourteenth and Fifteenth Amendments were to bring former slaves into citizenship and guarantee their voting rights. Also a series of civil rights statutes were enacted by Congress to bring about social assimilation. Yet the national commitment to civil rights faltered by narrow judicial interpretation of civil rights laws, and significantly with the Plessy v. Ferguson Supreme Court decision which held that legal (de jure) segregation was constitutionally permissible.

A number of states enacted statutes or added constitutional provisions to restrict or bar blacks from exercising influence in politics. Grandfather clauses, white primaries, poll taxes, and literacy tests were all used effectively. Eventually court action, constitutional amendments, and congressional action restricted or prohibited these forms of legal discrimination.

Near the mid-twentieth century national attitudes concerning segregation and discrimination began to change and in this is reflected in Supreme Court decisions in 1950. However, legislation to end discrimination in state voting laws did not materialize until the civil rights laws of the 1960's. The Voting Rights Act of 1965 and its subsequent updates in 1970, 1975, and 1982 all have been effective in guaranteeing the rights of all citizens to vote.

CHAPTER SUMMARY (cont.)

Discrimination in education was dealt a severe blow by the Brown v. Board of Education Supreme Court decision of 1954, which effectively reversed the 1896 Plessy v. Ferguson precedent. In 1964, the Congress enacted the Civil Rights Act of 1964 which prohibited federal funds from being used by state and local governments that engaged in school discrimination. By the late 1970's the greatest school segregation existed outside the South.

The Civil Rights Act of 1964 also prohibited discrimination in hotels, motels, restaurants and further outlawed discrimination in employment.

Since the 1964 Civil Rights Act, there have been various government policies to overcome discrimination. Affirmative action programs have been used to recruit minorities and women for jobs and promotions. Quotas and ratios have been put into effect in various cases. Such policies are controversial and have met stiff resistance and criticism as discriminatory. However the Supreme Court has held in a series of cases that affirmative action programs can be permissible to overcome discrimination.

The struggle for racial equality reignited the struggle of American women for equality and led to Congress proposing an Equal Rights Amendment to the U. S. Constitution. This proposal failed in state ratification battles and yet congressional legislation as the Civil Rights Act of 1964, Equal Employment Opportunities Act of 1972 and Title IX of the Educational Amendment of 1972 have all been used to fight discrimination against women. The Supreme Court in Roe v. Wade struck down state laws prohibiting women from obtaining abortions in the first two trimesters of pregnancy, and women's rights groups have interpreted this as a victory for women by giving women control over their reproductive organs. However, this decision has been highly controversial and Congress has prohibited federal aid from being used to pay for abortions, while many states have unsuccessfully tried to enact legislation regulating abortions.

The Supreme Court has interpreted the Constitution as prohibiting discrimination on the basis of race by saying that racial distinctions in government policy actions are automatically suspect of being unconstitutional. Yet the Court has interpreted government policy actions based on sex as being constitutionally permissible if such sex classification standards serve government objectives. Thus government, under certain conditions, may treat people differently based on gender if such treatment serves

CHAPTER SUMMARY (cont.)

government purposes such as a military draft for men, but not for women.

One may conclude that this society has made significant strides to end discrimination based on race and sex and yet disparities and conditions of inequality continue to affect American society.

PRACTICE EXERCISES

FILL IN THE BLANKS

1. In the _____ _____ decision of 1857 the Supreme Court held that slaves were property and could be taken anywhere in the union.

2. The _____ _____ of 1863 freed slaves in states that were in rebellion against the union.

3. In the _____ ___ _____ case of 1896 the Supreme Court held segregation as constitutionally permissible.

4. Laws with clauses to permit people to vote if their grandfather had voted before 1870 were called _____ _____.

5. Taxes which were paid as a requirement for voting were called _____ _____.

6. In 1965 Congress adopted the _____ _____ _____ which restricted state government voter registration devices used to deny blacks the right to vote.

7. In 1954 the Supreme Court in the _____ ____ _____ _____ _____ case declared separate but equal segregation unconstitutional.

8. Segregation by deliberate government policy is called _____ _____ segregation.

9. A term used to describe policies and programs especially established to recruit and promote minorities and females in jobs and education is _____ _____.

10. In the Supreme Court case _____ ____ _____ a Texas law prohibiting abortion was declared unconstitutional.

91

MULTIPLE CHOICE

11. One of the oldest and most powerful organizations which has supported women's rights is the:
    a. Urban League
    b. National Jewish Congress
    c. National Organization of Women
    d. Planned Parenthood

12. Which of the following tests is often used by the Supreme Court to determine if laws based on sex are constitutionally permissible?
    a. suspect
    b. reasonable
    c. substantiality
    d. strict

13. Civil rights are different from civil liberties in that civil rights:
    a. involve the right not to be discriminated against because of race, color, or national origin
    b. involve the right of individuals to free speech
    c. are not guaranteed under the Constitution
    d. there are no distinctions

14. Which of the following amendments to the Constitution contains an equal protection clause which has been substantially used to attack discrimination?
    a. Thirteenth Amendment
    b. Fourteenth Amendment
    c. Fifteenth Amendment
    d. Twenty-sixth Amendment

15. Which of the following Supreme Court decisions held segregation constitutional?
    a. Brown v. Board of Education
    b. Plessy v. Ferguson
    c. Dred Scott v. Sanford
    d. McCulloch v. Maryland

16. Which of the following amendments to the Constitution attempted to outlaw voter discrimination based on race?
    a. Thirteenth Amendment
    b. Fourteenth Amendment
    c. Fifteenth Amendment
    d. Twenty-fifth Amendment

MULTIPLE CHOICE (cont.)

17. This device was used to prohibit persons from voting by permitting political parties to hold "private elections" by restricting party membership based on race. This device was the:
    a. Poll tax
    b. Grandfather clause
    c. Literacy test
    d. The white primary

18. In which of the following cases did the Supreme Court strike down laws prohibiting blacks from entering white law schools?
    a. Sweatt v. Painter
    b. Brown v. Board of Education
    c. Plessy v. Ferguson
    d. United Steel Workers v. Webber

19. Segregation which is based on housing patterns or private action rather than government action is called:
    a. de jure segregation
    b. de facto segregation
    c. Illegal and requiring government remedies
    d. Unusual and rarely existing

20. The Civil Rights Act of 1964 outlawed discrimination in jobs, motels, hotels, and contained some provisions on voting rights. The law is based on which of the following sections of the Constitution?
    a. Article II, Section 2
    b. Article IV, Section 2
    c. Article I, Section 8
    d. Fourteenth Amendment

TRUE OR FALSE

21. The Equal Rights Amendment was ratified and added to the Constitution in 1982. _____

22. The Supreme Court has held that federal laws may permit the military draft for men and this is not sexual discrimination. _____

23. The Supreme Court uses the suspect test to determine if laws treating men and women differently are constitutional. _____

24. The Supreme Court has held that affirmative action programs are constitutionally permissible. _____

93

TRUE OR FALSE (cont.)

25. The Missouri Compromise extended slavery into new states and territories as the new nation expanded westward. _____

DISCUSSION, ESSAY

I. Discuss major legislative acts and judicial decisions which have been used to end racial discrimination in jobs, education and public accommodations.

II. Discuss the arguments for and against affirmative action.

III. Discuss the struggle to end discrimination in voting rights.

IV. Discuss various devices and judicial decisions used to enforce segregation.

V. Discuss the approach that the Supreme Court has taken in dealing with issues relating to sex-based discrimination.

13 THE NATURE OF PUBLIC POLICY

CHAPTER OVERVIEW

Much of the work of government involves making and carrying out public policy and this chapter examines various aspects of the public policy process. Public policy is defined, factors that shape policymaking are explored, the stages of policymaking are described, characteristics of policymaking are stated and lastly, types of public policy are identified and explained.

LEARNING OBJECTIVES

1. Define and learn new terms and concepts relating to public policy.

2. Understand what is public policy.

3. Discuss the factors and stages of policymaking.

4. Recognize characteristics of policymaking.

5. Identify the types of public policy.

6. Distinguish among regulatory, distributive, and redistributive policies of government.

7. Comprehend the two types of defense policy.

8. Recognize elements of continuity and change in policymaking.

CHAPTER OUTLINE

I. What is Public Policy
   A. Definition
   B. Purpose of policy analysis

CHAPTER OUTLINE (cont.)

II. Making and Developing Public Policy
   A. Factors that shape policymaking
      1. Actors and interests
      2. Beliefs and traditions
      3. Formal rules, procedures
   B. Stages of policymaking
      1. Setting the policy agenda
      2. Formulating and adopting policies
      3. Implementing policies
      4. Evaluating the impact of policies
      5. Terminating policies

III. Characteristics of Policy Making
   A. Fragmentation
   B. Decentralization
   C. Incrementalism
   D. Lack of information available
   E. Diffusion of authority over policymaking

IV. Types of Public Policy
   A. Domestic policy
      1. Regulatory policy
         a. Competitive
         b. Protective
      2. Distributive policy
      3. Redistributive policy
   B. Foreign policy
   C. Defense policy
   D. Crisis policy

CHAPTER SUMMARY

Policies of government affect our lives on a routine, daily basis. All levels of government establish programs, pursue government objectives, and shape our lives and opportunities in many ways. Federal actions concerning health programs, farm programs, defense and foreign policy are examples of public policy. A number of political scientists are concerned with analyzing public policy in order to provide information as to the nature of public policy, the reasons and forces which influence government to develop policies, and finally an analysis of the results, intentional and unintentional, of governmental policy.

Making public policy can be very complicated and there are three prominent factors which determine policymaking. These factors are: actors and interests that influence policy direction of government, beliefs and traditions that frame

96

CHAPTER SUMMARY (cont.)

the parameters of policy, and the rules, procedures, and institutions of government which are involved in administering, interpreting, and determining the constitutionality of policies.

It is important to understand policymaking in order to influence the process and there are at least five identifiable stages of policymaking. The stages are: to establish the policy agenda, to develop a policy proposal, to address a problem, to implement the policy, to evaluate the policy, and to terminate the policy.

Policymaking also has several recognizable characteristics, regardless of the specific policies developed. These characteristics are: fragmentation, decentralization, incrementalism, inadequate information, and finally, diffusion of control over the policymaking process.

Public policy can be classified into four major categories: domestic, foreign, defense, and crisis policy. Often times these policy areas can also be described by purpose as distributive policies, which attempt to encourage or promote activities, or regulatory policies, which involve government regulations of the private sector of the economy. There exists a third purpose classification, redistributive policies, which redistribute benefits or services among various groups in society.

Foreign policy is concerned with U. S. relations with foreign governments and may also use distributive and regulatory policies for established foreign policy goals.

Defense policy is concerned with national security and military needs and is often interrelated with foreign policy. Two classifications of defense policy are strategic defense policy and structural defense policy. Strategic policy refers to policy which identifies vital national interests and goals, and structural defense policy which often involves resource allocation necessary to successfully attain strategic goals.

In both foreign and defense policy areas, international emergencies and confrontations may suddenly develop. These sudden emergencies may result in short term crisis policy as a response to the emergency. Such crisis policy may not involve long term public dialogue and frequently the executive branch initiates the response to the emergency with Congress being consulted.

CHAPTER SUMMARY (cont.)

Regardless of the policy area or type of policy, one may conclude that usually new policies build upon the framework of existing policy. Also, policies do change and various interests and actors provide continuity but change as well.

PRACTICE EXERCISES

FILL IN THE BLANKS

1. Government programs and goals that range from setting speed limits to taxing people for energy conservation may be called _____ _____.

2. The set of issues and problems which government identifies and concerns itself with and is working on at any one time is called the_____ _____.

3. The stage of analyzing the consequences of public policy is called policy _____.

4. _____ regulatory policy is designed to protect the public and may include such things as warning labels on cigarette packages.

5. _____ are a form of distributive policy that offer benefits to encourage certain goals of commodities for society.

6. Aid to Families with Dependent Children (AFDC) policy is a form of _____ policy.

7. _____ defense policies are concerned with the draft and how reserve or national guard forces are to be deployed.

8. _____ policy establishes and determines relations of the United States with other countries.

9. _____ defense policy sets forth broad goals of protecting vital interests and locations of U.S. military forces abroad.

10. Perhaps the most difficult stage of policymaking is the stage of policy _____.

MULTIPLE CHOICE

11. A subcategory of defense and foreign policy which usually involves a response to a sudden or unexpected emergency in international relations is:
    a. foreign policy
    b. strategic defense policy
    c. distributive foreign policy
    d. crisis policy

12. Which of the following would be an example of public policy?
    a. a company decision to increase profit margins
    b. a farmer deciding to buy a cow
    c. a child deciding to eat a pizza
    d. a government regulation of cheese content in pizza

13. In order, the stages of policymaking are:
    a. agenda setting, policy formulation and adoption, evaluating policy, implementing policy, and terminating policy
    b. policy formulation and adoption, agenda setting, evaluating policy, implementing policy and terminating policy
    c. agenda setting, policy formulation and adoption, implementing policy, evaluating policy, and policy termination
    d. agenda setting, evaluating policy, policy formulation and adoption, implementing policy, and terminating policy

14. Often policies are simply added to existing policy. This is referred to as:
    a. incrementalism
    b. fragmentation
    c. decentralization
    d. diffusion

15. For a government to permit one company to provide exclusive electric service is an example of:
    a. domestic redistributive policy
    b. protective regulatory policy
    c. competitive regulatory policy
    d. domestic distributive policy

16. "Pork barrel" legislation generally takes the form of:
    a. domestic distributive policy
    b. domestic redistributive policy
    c. protective regulatory policy
    d. structural defense policy

MULTIPLE CHOICE (cont.)

17. Foreign aid to different countries is an example of
    a. strategic defense policy
    b. regulatory foreign policy
    c. distributive foreign policy
    d. structural defense policy

18. Placing trade sanctions against the Republic of South Africa is an example of:
    a. strategic defense policy
    b. regulatory foreign policy
    c. distributive foreign policy
    d. structural defense policy

19. Policy which determines the placement of missiles and military assistance given to allies is an example of:
    a. strategic defense policy
    b. regulatory foreign policy
    c. distributive foreign policy
    d. structural defense policy

20. Often policies are carried out by many different agencies and involve many different levels of authority. This characteristic of policymaking is called:
    a. incrementalism
    b. fragmentation
    c. decentralization
    d. centralization

TRUE OR FALSE

21. Policy termination is usually easy and prompt. _____

22. Tax and spending policies are examples of economic policy. _____

23. Policies as welfare benefits and food stamps are examples of redistributive policy. _____

24. The final stage of policy formulation is policy adoption. _____

25. Safety requirements in mines and factories are examples of protective regulatory policies. _____

DISCUSSION, ESSAY

I. Identify and describe classifications of public policies.

II. Identify and describe characteristics of policymaking.

III. Discuss the process of policymaking.

IV. Discuss three factors that shape policymaking.

V. Identify and describe five stages in policymaking.

14 ANSWER KEY

ANSWER KEY FOR PRACTICE EXERCISES

CHAPTER 1

FILL IN THE BLANKS

1. who gets what, when, how
2. pluralism, elitism
3. direct democracy
4. social contract
5. American creed
6. tradition, charisma, legality
7. public policy
8. republican government
9. self-government
10. liberty

MULTIPLE CHOICE

11. d
12. b
13. a
14. d
15. c
16. b
17. b
18. a
19. b
20. d

TRUE OR FALSE

21. True
22. False
23. True
24. True
25. False

CHAPTER 2

FILL IN THE BLANKS

1. English Bill of Rights
2. Second Continental Congress
3. Articles of Confederation
4. Shay's Rebellion
5. Virginia
6. Connecticut Compromise
7. federalism
8. judicial review
9. checks and balances
10. Federalist Papers

MULTIPLE CHOICE

11. c
12. b
13. a
14. b
15. d
16. a
17. c
18. b
19. d
20. a

TRUE OR FALSE

21. False
22. True
23. True
24. False
25. False

CHAPTER 3

FILL IN THE BLANKS

1. unitary
2. confederation
3. McCulloch v. Maryland
4. bills of attainder
5. reserved powers
6. dual federalism
7. creative federalism
8. block grants
9. revenue sharing
10. interstate compacts

MULTIPLE CHOICE

11. b
12. d
13. a
14. c
15. d
16. a
17. c
18. b
19. c
20. d

TRUE OR FALSE

21. True
22. False
23. False
24. True
25. True

CHAPTER 4

FILL IN THE BLANKS

1. political culture
2. political socialization
3. political opinion
4. intensity
5. sample
6. Oregon v. Mitchell
7. bandwagon
8. agenda setting
9. Twenty-sixth
10. responsive-voter

MULTIPLE CHOICE

11. d
12. b
13. c
14. b
15. c
16. a
17. b
18. b
19. d
20. a

TRUE OR FALSE

21. True
22. False
23. False
24. True
25. False

CHAPTER 5

FILL IN THE BLANKS

MULTIPLE CHOICE

1. nominating candidates
2. interest (pressure) groups
3. precinct
4. social consensus
5. South
6. national convention
7. dealignment
8. realignment
9. single issue
10. Brown v. Board of Education of Topeka

11. d
12. c
13. c
14. d
15. b
16. b
17. c
18. a
19. b
20. a

TRUE OR FALSE

21. True
22. False
23. False
24. False
25. True

CHAPTER 6

FILL IN THE BLANKS

MULTIPLE CHOICE

1. open
2. caucus
3. Wisconsin
4. super delegates
5. Republican, Democratic
6. permanent
7. straight ticket
8. gerrymandering
9. incumbents
10. rose garden

11. b
12. d
13. d
14. a
15. c
16. a
17. b
18. d
19. d
20. c

TRUE OR FALSE

21. False
22. False
23. True
24. True
25. False

CHAPTER 7

FILL IN THE BLANKS   MULTIPLE CHOICE

1. authorization, appropriation   11. c
2. Budget and Impoundment Control Act   12. b
3. Balanced Budget and Emergency Control Act   13. d
4. reapportionment   14. a
5. President of the Senate   15. b
6. standing   16. a
7. conference   17. d
8. seniority   18. c
9. private   19. d
10. Committee of the Whole   20. b

TRUE OR FALSE

21. True
22. False
23. False
24. True
25. False

CHAPTER 8

FILL IN THE BLANKS   MULTIPLE CHOICE

1. Spiro Agnew   11. b
2. majority, two-thirds   12. d
3. executive agreement   13. d
4. item veto   14. b
5. active-negative   15. c
6. passive-negative   16. d
7. chief of state   17. c
8. riders   18. c
9. party leader   19. b
10. War Powers Resolution   20. a

TRUE OR FALSE

21. False
22. True
23. False
24. True
25. True

CHAPTER 9

FILL IN THE BLANKS

1. traditional
2. charismatic
3. line
4. bureau
5. corporation
6. Executive Office of the President
7. spoils
8. Senate
9. iron triangle
10. oversight

MULTIPLE CHOICE

11. d
12. a
13. b
14. d
15. b
16. c
17. a
18. d
19. c
20. c

TRUE OR FALSE

21. False
22. False
23. True
24. True
25. False

CHAPTER 10

FILL IN THE BLANKS

1. Original intent
2. judicial activism
3. administrative law
4. civil
5. adversary
6. statutory
7. jurisdiction
8. legislative
9. misdemeanor
10. concurring

MULTIPLE CHOICE

11. d
12. c
13. b
14. b
15. c
16. a
17. c
18. c
19. b
20. d

TRUE OR FALSE

21. True
22. True
23. False
24. True
25. False

108

CHAPTER 11

FILL IN THE BLANKS

1. establishment clause
2. prior restraint
3. sedition
4. Miller v. California
5. symbolic
6. bill of attainder
7. Fourth
8. Mapp v. Ohio
9. Katz v. United States
10. grand

MULTIPLE CHOICE

11. d
12. b
13. c
14. d
15. b
16. a
17. b
18. d
19. a
20. d

TRUE OR FALSE

21. False
22. False
23. True
24. True
25. True

CHAPTER 12

FILL IN THE BLANKS

1. Dred Scott
2. Emancipation Proclamation
3. Plessy v. Ferguson
4. Grandfather clause
5. poll taxes
6. Voting Rights Act
7. Brown v. Board of Education
8. de jure
9. affirmative action
10. Roe v. Wade

MULTIPLE CHOICE

11. c
12. c
13. a
14. b
15. b
16. c
17. d
18. a
19. b
20. c

TRUE OR FALSE

21. False
22. True
23. False
24. True
25. False

CHAPTER 13

FILL IN THE BLANKS

1. public policy
2. policy agenda
3. evaluation
4. protective
5. subsidies
6. redistributive
7. structural
8. foreign
9. strategic
10. termination

MULTIPLE CHOICE

11. d
12. d
13. c
14. a
15. c
16. a
17. c
18. b
19. a
20. b

TRUE OR FALSE

21. False
22. True
23. True
24. True
25. True